ZAKHOR

Jewish History and Jewish Memory

YOSEF HAYIM YERUSHALMI

FOREWORD BY HAROLD BLOOM

With a New Preface and Postscript by the Author

SCHOCKEN BOOKS · NEW YORK

◪

Library of Congress Cataloging-in-Publication Data

Yerushalmi, Yosef Hayim, 1932–
Zakhor, Jewish history and Jewish memory.

Reprint. Originally published: Seattle : University
of Washington Press, © 1982. Originally published in
series: The Samuel and Althea Stroum lectures in
Jewish studies.
Includes index.
1. Jews—Historiography.   I. Title.
DS115.5.Y47   1989   909'.04924'0072   88-43130
ISBN 0-8052-0878-X

Cover art and title page illustrations:
Jews reading the Book of Lamentations in the synagogue on the 9th of Ab, the
annual commemoration of the destruction of the Temple in Jerusalem (from *Sefer
Minhagim,* Amsterdam, 1723).

Display type by Fearn Cutler
Manufactured in the United States of America

To the memory of

my father

YEHUDA YERUSHALMI

for the loving gift of a living past

and to my son

ARIEL

who brings joy to the present

and past into future

THE SAMUEL AND ALTHEA STROUM LECTURES
IN JEWISH STUDIES

Samuel Stroum, businessman, community leader, and philanthropist, by a major gift to the Jewish Federation of Greater Seattle, established the Samuel and Althea Stroum Philanthropic Fund.

In recognition of Mr. and Mrs. Stroum's deep interest in Jewish history and culture, the Board of Directors of the Jewish Federation of Seattle, in cooperation with the Jewish Studies Program of the University of Washington, established an annual lectureship at the University of Washington known as the Samuel and Althea Stroum Lectureship in Jewish Studies. This lectureship makes it possible to bring to the area outstanding scholars and interpreters of Jewish thought, thus promoting a deeper understanding of Jewish history, religion, and culture. Such understanding can lead to an enhanced appreciation of the Jewish contributions to the historical and cultural traditions that have shaped the American nation.

The terms of the gift also provide for the publication from time to time of the lectures or other appropriate materials resulting from or related to the lectures.

CONTENTS

Foreword by Harold Bloom
xiii

Preface to the Schocken Edition
xxvii

Prologue
xxxiii

1. BIBLICAL AND RABBINIC FOUNDATIONS
Meaning in History, Memory, and the Writing of History
I

2. THE MIDDLE AGES
Vessels and Vehicles of Jewish Memory
27

3. IN THE WAKE OF THE SPANISH EXPULSION
53

4. MODERN DILEMMAS
Historiography and Its Discontents
77

Postscript: Reflections on Forgetting
105

Notes
118

Index
147

For inquire, I pray thee, of the former generation,
And apply thyself to that which their fathers
   have searched out—
For we are but of yesterday, and know nothing,
Because our days upon earth are a shadow—
Shall not they teach thee, and tell thee,
And utter words out of their heart?
                                                —Job 8:8

having known this fate of ours so well
wandering around among broken stones, three or six
   thousand years
searching in collapsed buildings that might have been
   our homes
trying to remember dates and heroic deeds:
will we be able?
                        —George Seferis, *Mythistorema*, no. 22

Foreword

BY HAROLD BLOOM

I

Leo Strauss, political philosopher and Hebraic sage, in 1962
wrote a long preface for the English translation of his *Spinoza's
Critique of Religion.* Brooding on his book's genesis some thirty-
five years after its composition, Strauss was moved to write his
own intellectual elegy for German Jewry. In some sense, that
preface is a classical essay on "Jewish History and Jewish Memory," the subtitle of Yosef Hayim Yerushalmi's eloquent and
disturbing book. *Zakhor,* the title, is the verb used throughout the
Hebrew Bible whenever Israel is admonished: "Remember!"
Strauss, a touch more implicitly than the Bible, also admonished
us to remember:

> The establishment of the state of Israel is the most profound
> modification of the Galut [the Diaspora, or Exile] which has occur-
> red, but it is not the end of the Galut: in the religious sense, and
> perhaps not only in the religious sense, the state of Israel is a part of
> the Galut. Finite, relative problems can be solved; infinite, absolute
> problems cannot be solved . . . it looks as if the Jewish people were
> the chosen people in the sense, at least, that the Jewish problem is
> the most manifest symbol of the human problem as a social or politi-
> cal problem.

Surveying the tradition of the critique of religion, early in his
book on Spinoza, Strauss remarked on the Epicurean view of
history:

> Of past sorrows Epicurus takes no heed. He recalls his past only
> in so far as it is pleasurable. It is the decisive characteristic of the
> Epicurean that he is incapable of suffering from his past.

xiii

Nothing could be more un-Jewish, and one sees again why the great rabbis used "Epicurean" as a term of the greatest abuse. An Epicurean attitude toward memory is antithetical to Judaism. Yosef Hayim Yerushalmi is an exemplary Jewish historian of the Jews, and with *Zakhor* he becomes an exemplary theorist of the troubling and possibly irreconcilable split between Jewish memory and Jewish historiography. *Zakhor* is a small book, but it may well be a permanent contribution to Jewish speculation upon the dilemmas of Jewishness, and so it may join the canon of Jewish wisdom literature.

Yerushalmi, Salo Baron's successor at Columbia University, is deeply learned in all of Jewish history, but particularly so on the Marranos (the Sephardic Jews who were forced in the fifteenth century to convert to Christianity but continued secretly to maintain Jewish life), on the Inquisition, and indeed on all of Sephardic Jewry. The origin of *Zakhor* is an earlier essay by Yerushalmi, "Clio and the Jews," the crucial portions of which he has incorporated here. Reading his earlier books, one finds the reflective pattern that led him to *Zakhor. From Spanish Court to Italian Ghetto* chronicles the career of Isaac Cardoso, a seventeenth-century Marrano physician and defender of Judaism. The kernel of *Zakhor* is already present when Yerushalmi broods on the trauma of the Spanish expulsion of the Jews in 1492:

. . . it had raised the perennial problem of Jewish exile and suffering to a new level of urgency. Jews in the sixteenth century had groped for a new understanding of the ancient enigmas, and had responded with novel departures in historiography, mysticism, and messianism. In the seventeenth century the messianic passion stimulated earlier by the spread of Lurianic Kabbalah would finally erupt in the worldwide explosion of the Sabbatian movement, with its concomitant antinomian elements.

In his vast "panorama in facsimile of five centuries of the printed Haggadah," *Haggadah and History,* Yerushalmi denies that the celebration of Passover is merely a study of Jewish nostalgias, and instead affirms a kind of union between Jewish memory and Jewish history:

However dimly perceived, in the end it is nothing less than the Jewish experience and conception of history that are celebrated here. . . .

For Passover is preeminently the great historical festival of the Jewish people, and the Haggadah is its book of remembrance and redemption. Here the memory of the nation is annually renewed and replenished, and the collective hope sustained.

Jewish memory and Jewish history do not seem to have a vexed relationship here, but the reader can find the matter darkening in Yerushalmi's grimly impressive *The Lisbon Massacre of 1506.* His subject in this masterly monograph is the unhappy dialectic of Jewish existence by which the Jews of exile perpetually sought everywhere an alliance with the ruling powers, thus further provoking the hatred of already dangerous masses. As Yerushalmi observes, the pattern is prevalent as far back as Hellenistic times, and has its contemporary relevances, in support of which he cites the late Hannah Arendt's controversial second chapter in *The Origins of Totalitarianism,* "The Jews and Society." Though he did not say so, I surmise that Yerushalmi began to see in this unhappy pattern a prime instance of how Jewish memory and Jewish history fail to inform each other.

In *Between Past and Future,* Arendt made the most useful distinction I have found between the Greek concept of history and the Hebrew rejection of such a concept. Greek historiography, like Greek poetry, is concerned with greatness: "Through history men almost became the equals of nature, and only those events, deeds, or words that rose by themselves to the ever-present challenge of the natural universe were what we would call historical." Against this historiography was Jewish memory, based "upon the altogether different teaching of the Hebrews, who always held that life itself is sacred, more sacred than anything else in the

world, and that man is the supreme being on earth." Memory, as
Arendt taught elsewhere, can be a powerful mode of cognition,
and with this teaching one can begin a reading of Yerushalmi's
Zakhor.

Zakhor is divided into four chapters, tracing in turn the for-
tunes of Jewish memory and Jewish history in their Biblical and
rabbinical origins, in the Middle Ages, in the wake of the Spanish
Expulsion, and in our time. All four chapters are remarkable, but
I find the first the most memorable. Yerushalmi begins by empha-
sizing that "only in Israel and nowhere else is the injunction to
remember felt as a religious imperative to an entire people." But
is there a peculiar or particular Hebrew psychology of memory?
The first book mentioned in Yerushalmi's notes is *Memory and
Tradition in Israel* by Brevard S. Childs (London, 1962), which
decides against the idea of a uniquely Hebraic mode of memory
while also insisting that *zakhor,* as a word, has a much wider range
than "remember" has in English, since in Hebrew to remember
is also to act (a parallel to the Hebrew *davar,* translated as *logos*
but meaning "act" and "thing" as well as "word").

Yerushalmi shrewdly emphasizes the uniquely selective nature of Hebrew memory, which calls for a particular kind of
acting rather than for any curiosity about the past: "Israel is told
only that it must be a kingdom of priests and a holy people;
nowhere is it suggested that it become a nation of historians."
Heroic individuals or even national deeds do not matter, and
Yerushalmi notes that many Biblical narratives are scandals or
disgraces if judged on the basis of their likely effect upon national pride. God's acts and Israel's responses matter, and nothing else. If that is what matters, then the priest and the prophet
become the masters of memory and historians become unlikely
figures. And yet so much of the Bible is distinguished historical
narrative, narrative that is human in scale, concrete in fact and
detail, mostly chronological, and rarely as fictive or legendary as
it may look. This paradox prompts one of Yerushalmi's central
formulations:

. . . meaning in history, memory of the past, and the writing of history are by no means to be equated. In the Bible, to be sure, the three elements are linked, they overlap at critical points, and, in general, they are held together in a web of delicate and reciprocal relationships. In post-biblical Judaism, as we shall see, they pull asunder. Even in the Bible, however, historiography is but one expression of the awareness that history is meaningful and of the need to remember, and neither meaning nor memory ultimately depends upon it. The meaning of history is explored more directly and more deeply in the prophets than in the actual historical narratives; the collective memory is transmitted more actively through ritual than through chronicle.

Prophet and priest deal in sacred history, and when the canon of the Bible was closed by the rabbis, at about the year 100 of the Common Era, then the Jews seem almost to have stopped writing even sacred history. The works of Josephus, written between the late seventies and the early nineties of the first century C.E., vanished from among the Jews. Yerushalmi remarks that "it would be almost fifteen centuries before another Jew would actually call himself an historian." The rabbis who founded the Judaism that we know, the religion of Akiba, lost all interest in mundane history. They had the written and the oral law, and they trusted in the covenant, which assured them the future. Roman history, Parthian history, even the contemporary Jewish history of the Hasmoneans and the Herodians, were scarcely worthy of rabbinical scrutiny.

When the great Akiba, as an old man, proclaimed Bar Kochba the Messiah, helping thus to bring on the great massacres by the Romans, the Jewish disaster of the second century C.E., he gave his rabbinical colleagues the last encouragement they needed to forget contemporary history forever. After that, as Yerushalmi strongly says, the rabbis "obviously felt they had all the history they required." Judaism kept its belief in the meaning of history while teaching habits of thought that were and are profoundly ahistorical. A Jew might be a poet or a philosopher or a kabbalist speculator as well as a rabbi, but for fifteen centuries he would not think of being a historian.

In his second chapter, on the transmission of Jewish memory in the Middle Ages, Yerushalmi remarks that even the ahistorical character of rabbinic thinking in itself cannot account for medieval Jewry's sense that reading or writing history was merely what Maimonides called it, a "waste of time." Jewish memory moved instead through ritual and liturgy, and in rabbinic custom and law, fairly well fixed after the year 500 C.E., when the Talmud achieved its definitive form. Yerushalmi identifies four particular vehicles of medieval Jewish memory: new penitential prayers inserted into the liturgy; "memorial books" in each community; "Second Purims," to celebrate fresh deliverance; and special fast days, for the catastrophes from which there had been no deliverance. Together with the modes of spiritual creativity open to medieval Jewry—*halakhah* (law), kabbalah, and philosophy—these modes of memory subsumed all the possibilities of history.

In the sixteenth century, in the wake of the Spanish Expulsion, suddenly some of the Jews turned to historical writing again, a resurgence that Yerushalmi addresses in his third chapter. His conclusion, though, is that this phenomenon was ephemeral and abruptly faded away, in sharp contrast to the other great intellectual reaction of exiled Iberian Jewry, the Lurianic Kabbalah, which rapidly spread from Safed, in Galilee, to dominate Jewish spiritual life almost everywhere. Gnostic myth, and not history, provided the extra strength that Jewish memory needed for Jewry to survive its latest catastrophe. Yerushalmi is precise on the triumph of Kabbalah:

Clearly, the bulk of Jewry was unprepared to tolerate history in immanent terms. It is as though, with the culminating tragedy of the expulsion from Spain, Jewish history had become opaque, and could not yield a satisfactory meaning even when, as among most of the historians, it was viewed religiously. Patently, however, Jews were spiritually and psychologically prepared for that which Lurianic Kabbalah afforded them—a mythic interpretation of history that lay beyond history. . . .

What remains then for Yerushalmi, in his last chapter, is what he aptly calls "Modern Dilemmas," with the quasi-Freudian subtitle "Historiography and Its Discontents," since modern Jewish historians are not the heirs of the rabbis or the kabbalists, but rather of Barthold Niebuhr and Leopold von Ranke. That is to say (though Yerushalmi does not say it), that historiography, of all the modern disciplines practiced by Jewish scholars, is necessarily the most Gentile. But that is not in itself a major discontent, since Yerushalmi rightly observes that "the primary intellectual encounter between Judaism and modern culture has lain precisely in a mutual preoccupation with the historicity of things." With Jewish group memory now in sharp decay, "history becomes what it had never been before—the faith of fallen Jews." And there Yerushalmi locates one of the discontents both in the nineteenth century and now. Scripture has been replaced by history as the validating arbiter of Jewish ideologies, and the replacement, he believes, has yielded chaos.

Yerushalmi goes on to trace deeper discontents in contemporary Jewish historiography, which he sees as standing in opposition to its own subject matter, since it cannot credit God's will as the active cause behind Jewish events, and it cannot regard Jewish history as being unique. Spinoza, as interpreted by Leo Strauss, is thus, after all, the only Jewish precursor of modern Jewish historiography, which has followed him in secularizing what had been sacred history. A further discontent, also prophesied by Spinoza, now becomes evident: Judaism itself has been historicized, by Gentile and Jewish historians alike. With that process well advanced, Jewish memory and Jewish history begin to oppose each other, and there Yerushalmi finds his crucial dilemma.

The total coherence of a scholarly Jewish history, whatever that will turn out to be, will be very different from the lost coherence of Jewish memory at its strongest, which was messianic and therefore redemptive. Literature and ideology compete to occupy the abyss that Jewish memory has become; Jewish historical research, as Yerushalmi admits, has no effect upon contemporary Jewish visions of the past. The Jews, now as before, remain fundamen-

tally ahistorical. Yerushalmi wryly says of them that they "await
a new, metahistorical myth, for which the novel provides at least
a temporary modern surrogate." Post-Holocaust Jewry, Yerushalmi concludes, resembles the generations that followed the
Spanish Expulsion, and so also will choose myth over history.

Perhaps Yerushalmi, for all his realism, is too hopeful. Contemporary Jewish novelists and ideologues seem to me simply not
strong enough to replace lost Jewish memory. The late Gershom
Scholem was the closest equivalent to a modern Isaac Luria that
we had, but he deliberately and evasively carried his scholarship
only to the borders of a new myth of exile, and finally did not dare
to cross over from history to a redemptive messianic hope. We
do not know, Scholem said, why certain sparks survived, even
while so much of Jewry fell away. Perhaps the myth or myths that
yet will rekindle Jewish memory, here in the West, can be found
in the lives and works of Freud and Kafka, and in Scholem's also.
We do not know.

The Jews were a religion that became a people, rather than a
people that became a religion. We will not know what is or is not
contemporary Jewish culture until we can examine it retrospec-
tively. Freud, Kafka, and Scholem may yet seem as much high
Jewish culture as we have had in this century. Yerushalmi's wisdom is most relevant and welcome when he urges the modern
Jewish historian to "understand the degree to which he himself
is a product of rupture." But this is true also of all modern Jewish
intellectuals. As Yerushalmi says, once aware of this, we are not
only bound to accept it, but we will be free to use it.

II

In the six years since I first read *Zakhor,* I have discovered
traces of it in my own meditations upon Freud, Kafka, and Gershom Scholem, as in all of my incessant broodings upon Jewish
culture and Jewish identity. Yerushalmi, starting from a strict
consideration of the emergence of modern Jewish historical scholarship, uncovered some of the inevitable consequences of un-

derstanding that emergence "as an historical fact historically conditioned." This makes Yerushalmi akin to Richard Rorty, who has taught many of us what most philosophers decline to learn, which is that our individualities are contingent and must affirm contingency, a lesson first taught by Nietzsche and by Freud, according to their exegetes, but which Rorty wisely ascribes to the strong poets, who were there before Nietzsche and Freud, as those great speculators always admitted. Contingency, in the Nietzschean and Rortean sense, can be grasped only by poets, and not by philosophers, theologians, or historians, because only poets achieve self-creation by way of the recognition of contingency, whereas philosophers and historians lust to attain universality by transcending contingency. Yerushalmi, in my judgment, is unique among Jewish historians in taking up the Nietzschean, or strong poetic, stance toward the contingency of what might be called modern Jewish selfhood. Rather than seeing that selfhood as being dependent upon an inherited vision of contingency, Yerushalmi insists upon our freedom to know that the essential aspect of our Jewish contingency is rupture, or what Nietzsche would have called a trope of self-overcoming. Nietzsche understood how frightening such rupture is, but it is difficult for Jews not to see their own contingency as being peculiarly terrifying. How can any Jewish intellectual in the closing years of our century say "thus I willed it" to the Jewish past? Can a Jew be a strong poet, when the price of such poethood includes the will's revenge against time and against time's "it was"? Cynthia Ozick has argued that the Talmudic sense of the virtues of the fathers and the mothers necessarily excludes any Jewish concept of belatedness, of needing to revise the precursors into shapes more available to us. Ozick herself nevertheless becomes a strong storyteller, as she knows, only when she reforges her own convictions of Jewish contingency, in "Envy, or Yiddish in America," "Usurpation," and *The Messiah of Stockholm,* narratives that do cry out "thus I willed it" to Jewish memory and to Jewish history. Ozick, despite her moral pain at affronting her own normative vision, develops her Nietzschean and Freudian self as another

picnic of contingencies, raised to strength only through a pragmatic perspectivism.

Yerushalmi clearly recognizes his own Nietzschean perspectivism, yet might be a touch rueful at contemplating his own American Jewish version of pragmatism, or idiosyncratic contingency,
as Emerson and Rorty want us to call it. The psychology of
belatedness, being unsparing, involves *Zakhor* deeply in the
dilemmas of Jewish historiography that it so accurately describes.
As Yerushalmi observes, the dilemma centers upon ruptures,
breaks in continuity with many aspects of the Jewish past. I would
suggest that the discontinuities always have been there, throughout Jewish history, and that the difference now centers upon our
consciousness of disruption. The largest figures in modern Jewish
culture are Freud and Kafka, neither of whom was embedded
within the traditions of normative Judaism. Freud and Kafka thus
become the hidden presences in *Zakhor,* because their eminence
is the context out of which Yerushalmi knowingly writes.

The distinction of *Zakhor* as history-writing opens up again the
whole question of modern Jewish writing. Is it a definable entity,
with characteristics of its own? You cannot decide whether modern Jewish writing possesses common elements without defining
the undecidable issue of who is or is not Jewish. Is Proust somehow a Jewish writer? If he was, then what about Montaigne?
Clearly Jewish ancestry is hardly in itself a sufficient cause of
Jewish writing, nor can we associate Jewish imagination with
normative Judaism. By common consent, Kafka is not only the
strongest modern Jewish writer, but *the* Jewish writer. His only
rival increasingly seems to be Freud, who, together with Kafka,
may yet redefine Jewish culture for us, and so change our sense
of Jewish memory.

American Jewish writing is haunted by Kafka; much the same
can be said of recent Israeli writing, though the haunting there
is considerably darker in its pathos. Compare, for instance, the
effect of Kafka on Philip Roth in *The Prague Orgy* to the Kafkan
influence in Yehoshua or in Appelfeld. Roth's extraordinary hi-

Foreword xxiii

larity, the pained laughter he evokes, reminds us that Kafka's circle found uproariously funny the openings of "The Metamorphosis" and *The Trial*. Appelfeld and Yehoshua employ the Kafkan irreality in order to empty out their already emptied protagonists. Kafka contains both Philip Roth and Appelfeld; they cannot contain him, and are wise enough to know it. We perhaps can speak of them as Jewish writers because of their common Kafkan heritage, but they inherit different aspects of their precursor, and they make us reflect also that you scarcely need to be Jewish to be influenced by Kafka, or by Freud, for that matter.

Kafka and Freud are so strong and so Jewish that we redefine the Jewish on their basis, but what is it about them that is Jewish? I think that finally their Jewishness consists in their intense obsession with interpretation, as such. All Jewish writing tends to be outrageously interpretive, so that the Nietzschean question applies poorly to them—"Who is the interpreter, and what power does he seek to gain over the text?" You can discard Nietzsche's formulation when you interpret a Jewish interpretation, because the power sought over the text is then always the same: he seeks the blessing, so that his name will not be scattered, so that more life will be granted him into a time without boundaries. Kafka's Negative works so as to make interpretation of Kafka virtually impossible, but in turn that compels us to interpret why Kafka makes himself uninterpretable. Freud, by insisting that everything is meaningful, and can be interpreted, sets the other polarity of Jewish writing. Both show that there is sense in everything, and then in opposite ways negate the sense you might seek to find, a negation akin to Yerushalmi's antithesis of Jewish history and Jewish memory.

You don't have to be Jewish to be a compulsive interpreter, but, of course, it helps. What Jewish writing has to interpret, finally, and however indirectly, is the Hebrew Bible, since that always has been the function of Jewish writing, or rather its burden: how to open the Bible to one's own suffering. But then, the

Hebrew Bible, in contrast to the New Testament or the Koran, never has been closed; it does not end with Second Chronicles, or with the *Kuzari* of Judah Halevi, or with *The Great Wall of China* of Kafka, or with the *Three Essays on the Theory of Sexuality* of Freud. The desire to be Scripture is hardly in itself Jewish; Dante and Milton each believed himself to be uttering prophecy. But to trust that you join yourself to the Hebrew Bible by opening it further to your own pathos does seem to me a peculiarly Jewish ambition for a writer. A Kafkan parable may be more Biblical than a Freudian essay overtly attempts to be, but all of Freud's cultural works rewrite the Hebrew Bible, until we reach the terrible culmination in *Moses and Monotheism,* an involuntary self-parody on Freud's part.

Mimesis of essential nature is the classical burden of representation, but hardly the Jewish burden. Sometimes I conclude that Plato marks the authentic difference between the Hebrew Bible and normative Judaism, since the Judaism of second-century (C.E.) Palestine could not have come about without the immense influx of Platonic thought-forms carried along by Hellenization. If I seek for what made Platonism so attractive to the sages of the school of Akiba, Ishmael, and Tarphon, I come up with a disturbing answer. Platonic representation is super-mimetic, because its true agon is with Homer, whose priority Plato deeply resented. Normative Jewish representation learned a super-mimetic stance from Hellenism, even though the rabbis gloried in the priority of Torah. Instead of competing with Torah, they decided to open it to themselves, and then succeeded, so that nearly all subsequent Jewish writing has been commentary upon Scripture, however indirect in America or Israel today. Jews do not write the poems of their climate; they write poems of the desire to be different, the desire to be elsewhere. If Moshe Idel is right, and I suspect he is, then Kabbalah is the basic Jewish mode of writing, rather than a deviation, because Kabbalah reaches back through Gnosticism to antithetical elements that were primal in the ancient Jewish religion, elements that are super-mimetic because they reject essential nature. On that argument, we might speculate that the

second-century rabbinic sages Platonized because they felt, however unconsciously, that they had an agon with Torah, even as
Plato consciously had one with Homer. Beneath the revisions of
received Torah were the stories of the J writer, or Yahwist, and
the God of those stories was something of an uncanny being, even
as the Patriarchs in those stories were theomorphic beings. A
Platonic stance, hidden but pervasive, made possible modes of
interpretation that honored the literal meanings of Torah while
opening up all the other levels to a flux of commentary, pragmati-
cally agonistic though almost never agonistic in tone.

Does that not remain, beneath infinite disguises, the condition
of contemporary American Jewish writing and Israeli writing,
even as it was the condition of the New Kabbalah of Franz Kafka?
The shadow of the Hebrew Bible is dark upon every page written
by a consciously Jewish writer—even upon the pages of Sigmund
Freud, once you have cleared away the false lights that Freud
shrewdly generated. There is no literary text anywhere that is
nearly as strong as the Hebrew Bible. The *Iliad* is matched by the
Yahwist, and even the Yahwist, strongest writer and Great Original of the Hebrew Bible, is only one element in its endlessly
varied strength. Doubtless the Hebrew Bible is an immense
source of literary vitality to its inheritors, but doubtless also it is
too immense for those who come to it, and from it, so belatedly.
What holds together modern Jewish writing, whether it be in
Hebrew or in Yiddish, in German or in American English, is the
Jewish Bible. This holding together is an enclosure, and to be
enclosed is both a protection and a punishment, which is the
perpetual condition of modern Jewish writing. It is also the condition of Yerushalmi's superb meditation upon the contingencies of
Jewish history, a meditation that is of necessity contained within
the dilemmas of modern Jewish writing.

New Haven, Connecticut
November 1988

Preface to the Schocken Edition

When *Zakhor* was published in 1982 I expected it, at best, to reach a small audience, garner a few serious reviews, and—such is the nature of hope in the academy—attain a modest though brief *succès d'estime*. To my considerable surprise, the book rapidly made its way among ever widening circles of both scholars and lay readers, Jews and non-Jews alike, and has been translated into French, Italian, Hebrew, and German. Conferences on *Zakhor*, or on its major theme, have been held in Paris, at Wesleyan University, Boston University, and the University of Haifa. My shortest book has thus traveled farthest. Now, by virtue of the present edition, it is endowed with the possibility of a second life.

Whatever its intrinsic virtues, I can only explain the reception of *Zakhor* as being due to circumstances beyond itself—it appeared, so to speak, at the proverbial "right time." Though I had been working in complete isolation, upon my arrival in Paris, in December 1984, for a conference on "Mémoire et Histoire,"[1] I discovered that I was not alone in my preoccupation with the problematics of collective memory and the writing of history; it was only that I was apparently the first to raise some of the issues sharply and publicly. The best example I can give is the fact that, unknown to me while I was working on *Zakhor*, the distinguished French historian Pierre Nora had already initiated the magisterial collaborative project on French collective memory (or rather memories) entitled *Les lieux de mémoire*, of which four volumes have appeared and three are yet to come.[2] Though working with very different historical materials, Nora's conception of "lieux de mémoire" corresponds closely to what I have called in chapter 2 "vessels and vehicles of memory."[3] In this, as in other instances that could be cited, what seems like mere coincidence points to a cultural climate that was ripe for such efforts.

Discounting the reviewer who took my statement that the book is "part history, part confession and credo" to mean the one must exclude the other, criticism of *Zakhor* has been largely favorable. Two exceptions, however, should be mentioned.

Thus I have been chided for underestimating the historical consciousness of medieval Jews and for not comparing them, on this score, with their non-Jewish contemporaries. To this I can only reply that the failure of such critics to distinguish between historical consciousness and the actual recording and interpretation of historical events is to miss one of the essential premises of the book and part of the reason I wrote it. (See also, more explicitly, pp. 31–34, below.)

The graver charge, that *Zakhor* represents an indictment and repudiation of modern historical scholarship *per se,* leaves me baffled. I thought I had made it perfectly clear that my aim was only to separate historiography from collective memory, insisting that the one cannot substitute for the other. Certainly I have expressed some "discontents" with modern historical scholarship, but I assumed it would be sufficient to stress that I continue to devote my life to it. One would also imagine that any serious reader would readily comprehend that *Zakhor* itself could never have been written without the perspectives and methods of the very same modern critical historical scholarship which I am alleged by some to be renouncing.

I have mentioned these strictures merely for the sake of further clarification. I certainly claim no immunity to criticism and, in general, I have been treated far more gently than I expected. Partly for this reason I have thought it useful to add a recent paper to the present edition. On June 3, 1987, I participated in a conference held at the former monastery of Royaumont, together with Jacques Le Goff, Pierre Nora, Hans Mommsen, Nicole Loraux, Jean-Claude Milner, Henry Rousso, and others. The conference was devoted to "Usages de l'oubli" (The Uses of Forgetting); selected papers including my own have just been published under this title in Paris.[4] The English text of my paper is presented here as a postscript to *Zakhor.* I believe this to be appropriate. My "Reflections on Forgetting" are, at their core, a further exploration of collective memory through a meditation on its mirror image. The final section of the essay should, I trust, remove any lingering doubts as to where I stand on the importance of modern historical research.

The present text of *Zakhor* reproduces that of the first edition with no changes except for the correction of a minor lapse in my own memory. Funes in Borges's short story was, of course, an Uruguayan, not an Argentinian.

My warmest thanks to Bonny Fetterman, my editor at Schocken Books, through whose initiative the entire project has come into being.

I also wish to thank Harold Bloom for enhancing this edition with a special introduction. That *Zakhor* could evoke so kaleido-scopic a reading from a literary intelligence I have so long ad-mired while, at the same time, my own intentions have been understood and scrupulously respected, is for me an experience as moving as it is revelatory.

Columbia University   Y.H.Y.
5749/1988

Acknowledgments

My warm appreciation to the University of Washington, and especially to Professor Edward Alexander, for inviting me to deliver the 1980 Stroum Lectures; to Mr. and Mrs. Stroum whose endowment established the annual series; to Professor Joan Ullman and other members of the faculty for their gracious hospitality; and to Professor Michael Stanislawski, now my close colleague at Columbia, for indulging my every whim during my stay in Seattle. I am indebted to Malka Gold, my assistant at the Center for Israel and Jewish Studies, for typing the several drafts of the manuscript with her usual care and devotion, and to my students Joshua Gutoff and Russell Herman for their help in reading proofs. Naomi Pascal has made my association with the University of Washington Press a particularly happy one, and in Marilyn Trueblood I have found an exemplary editor. I thank the American Academy for Jewish Research and its secretary, Professor Isaac Barzilay, for allowing me to incorporate portions of my essay "Clio and the Jews," which appeared in the *Proceedings* of the Academy. Finally, I express my gratitude to the National Endowment for the Humanities, whose generous fellowship grant in 1976–77 afforded me the year of uninterrupted study and contemplation that made this book possible.

Y.H.Y.

Prologue

This little book, part history, part confession and credo, has come into being through several distinct stages, none of which anticipated the other. In 1977, while on sabbatical in Jerusalem, I delivered a lecture on sixteenth-century Jewish historiography to the faculties of the Institute of Jewish Studies at the Hebrew University. My choice of subject was prompted not only by its inherent fascinations, but by my feeling that a proper understanding of this particular phenomenon can provide a fulcrum with which to raise a number of issues concerning the place of historiography within Jewish civilization generally. Upon my return to the United States I was asked to contribute a paper to the forthcoming Jubilee Volume of the American Academy for Jewish Research. In response, I submitted a lightly expanded English version of my Hebrew lecture, now entitled "Clio and the Jews: Reflections on Jewish Historiography in the Sixteenth Century," which was published when the volume finally appeared in the fall of 1980. Both in the original lecture and in the published essay I managed to confine myself rather closely to the announced topic, though there were also some scattered hints concerning its larger implications.

The matter might well have rested there had I not received, in the meantime, the gracious invitation of the University of Washington to deliver the Stroum Lectures in April 1980. This suddenly seemed to me a propitious opportunity for a more expansive treatment, no longer limited to any single period, of the issues with which I was concerned. Still, I formulated the topic as "Jewish History and Jewish Memory" with some qualms. Four lectures on so broad a theme would obviously preclude the elaborate and subtle discussion that many of the ideas to be dealt with really deserve. Despite such misgivings, I decided to plunge ahead. The lectures were given. This book is the result.

If such, then, are the external circumstances that have brought it forth, its more vital origin lies in an effort to understand myself as a Jewish historian, not within the objective context of the global

scholarly enterprise, but within the inner framework of Jewish
history itself. With the former I have no particular problems—
that is, none that are not shared by historians in other fields. Given
that it is important to consume most of one's waking hours in the
study of the past, Jewish historical scholarship is as significant as
any other and its achievements are manifest. From the perspective
of Jewish history, however, it is different. At the very heart of this
book lies an attempt to understand what seemed a paradox to me
at one time—that although Judaism throughout the ages was
absorbed with the meaning of history, historiography itself played
at best an ancillary role among the Jews, and often no role at all;
and, concomitantly, that while memory of the past was always a
central component of Jewish experience, the historian was not its
primary custodian.

These significant dualities have often been obscured by rhetor-
ical flourishes and a certain semantic confusion. The Jews, after all,
have the reputation of being at once the most historically oriented
of peoples and as possessing the longest and most tenacious of
memories. Yet such accolades can be profoundly true or completely
false, depending upon what one means by "history" or "memory."
If they are not to be completely meaningless, we should at least
want to know what kind of history the Jews have valued, what, out
of their past, they chose to remember, and how they preserved,
transmitted, and revitalized that which was recalled. Our investigation along these lines will gradually reveal, I trust, how very
different the traditional concern of Jews with history was from
our own. This book, therefore, may properly be considered, on one
level, as an attempt at historical *distancing*.

My own terms of reference require no rigid definitions. They
should emerge, on the whole, with sufficient clarity in the contexts
that follow. I have discussed my understanding of "historiography"
at some length in the "Clio" essay, where I have also given examples of those who would blur the crucial distinction between
historical writing and various genres of Jewish literature that may
reflect a deep concern with history without displaying the least

interest in recording historical events. All that need not be repeated here.

It may help to point out, however, that in repeatedly employing such terms as "collective memory" or "group memory" I do not have in mind some vaguely genetic endowment, nor an innate psychic structure analogous to the Jungian archetypes. Contrary to a theory widely held as late as the seventeenth century, a child left in the forest to its own linguistic devices would not speak Hebrew spontaneously, not even if it were a Jewish *enfant sauvage*, and neither would it "remember" that Abraham journeyed from Ur to Canaan. Only the group can bequeath both language and a transpersonal memory. It was the abiding merit of Maurice Halbwachs, more than fifty years ago, to have insisted to psychologists and philosophers alike that even individual memory is structured through social frameworks, and, all the more, that collective memory is not a metaphor but a social reality transmitted and sustained through the conscious efforts and institutions of the group (see *Les cadres sociaux de la mémoire*, Paris, 1925, and his posthumously published *La mémoire collective*, Paris, 1950). My own use of the term is indebted to these works, in spirit if not always in substance. However, in attempting a specific examination of the dynamics of *Jewish* collective memory, I have found little help at hand. The categories generally invoked are usually not adequate to the Jewish case. What has been learned from the study of oral tradition, for example, will only partially apply to so literate and obstinately bookish a people. Notions of collective memory derived from the folklore and mythology of peasants or primitives are also of limited relevance when we consider how much of Jewish society and culture was molded, prior to modern times, by guiding elites. Significantly, Halbwachs himself devoted a chapter in the first of his aforementioned books to "La mémoire collective des groupes religieux" in which he referred exclusively to Christianity, while in the discussion of "La mémoire collective et la mémoire historique" in the latter work, it is the historical memory of a nation that is at issue. The Jews, however, have represented throughout their history a unique fusion of religion and peoplehood, and they cannot be grasped on either side of such dichotomies. The history of Jewish collective memory, as I have indicated in the first lecture, is yet to be explored. Here I have only tried to chart some possible routes to be followed.

Returning to these lectures after the lapse of more than a year in order to prepare them for publication, I was tempted more than once to rewrite them completely, or even to lay them aside and to write a full-scale and much larger work on the very same themes. Instead I did neither. I decided to retain the format, and hence also the tonality, of the lectures as they were originally given. Revisions have been minimal and largely cosmetic. What has been lost thereby in amplitude and subtlety will perhaps be compensated by the immediacy of words spoken in a living context. At the same time, despite some initial hesitation I have seen fit to add rather extensive notes to each lecture, persuaded by close friends and colleagues that these may be useful to students, and that they would enable me to qualify and nuance at least some points that, inevitably, have been too baldly stated in the lectures themselves.

Reviewing the whole, I am under no illusion that this book is anything more than a series of tentative probes into its subject. In the end, the stance I have taken emerges out of an acute awareness that there have been a number of alternative ways, each viable and with its own integrity, in which human beings have perceived and organized their collective pasts. Modern historiography is the most recent, but still only one of these, superior in some obvious respects, deficient and perhaps even inferior in others, gain and loss. Thus I regard the emergence of modern Jewish historical scholarship since the early nineteenth century, not as an ultimate triumph of historical progress, but as an historical fact historically conditioned, something to be taken with the utmost seriousness, but not to crow about. Nevertheless, the reader will not have understood me if he interprets the doubts and misgivings I express as meaning that I propose a return to prior modes of thought. Most of us do not have that choice. For better or worse, a particular and

unprecedented experience of time and history is ours, to be reflected upon, perhaps to be channelled in new directions. My final
conclusions are admittedly not sanguine. Neither, I think, are they
hopeless.

Wellfleet, Cape Cod   Yosef Hayim Yerushalmi
30 Ab 5741/August 30, 1981

1

BIBLICAL AND RABBINIC FOUNDATIONS

Meaning in History, Memory, and the Writing of History

For ask now of the days past, which were before thee, since the day that God created man upon the earth, and from the one end of heaven unto the other, whether there hath been any such thing as this great thing is, or hath been heard like it?

—Deuteronomy 4:32

R. Eleazar ben Azariah said: Behold, I am about seventy years old, and I have never been worthy to find a reason why the Exodus from Egypt should be mentioned at night-time, until Ben Zoma expounded it thus: It is stated—*That thou mayest remember the day when thou camest forth out of the land of Egypt all the days of thy life* (Deut. 16:3). Had the text said "the days of thy life" it would have meant only the days; but "*all* the days of thy life" includes the nights as well. The sages, however, say: "The days of thy life" refers to this world; "*all* the days of thy life" is to include the days of the Messiah.

—Mishnah *Berakhot* 1:5

The Hebrew *Zakhor*—"Remember"—announces my elusive theme. Memory is always problematic, usually deceptive, sometimes treacherous. Proust knew this, and the English reader is deprived of the full force of his title which conveys, not the blandly reassuring "Remembrance of Things Past" of the Moncrieff translation, but an initially darker and more anxious search for a time that has been lost. In the ensorcelled film of Alain Resnais the heroine quickly discovers that she cannot even be certain of what transpired "last year at Marienbad." We ourselves are periodically aware that memory is among the most fragile and capricious of our faculties.

Yet the Hebrew Bible seems to have no hesitations in commanding memory. Its injunctions to remember are unconditional, and even when not commanded, remembrance is always pivotal. Altogether the verb *zakhar* appears in its various declensions in the Bible no less than one hundred and sixty-nine times, usually with either Israel or God as the subject, for memory is incumbent upon both.[1] The verb is complemented by its obverse—forgetting. As Israel is enjoined to remember, so is it adjured not to forget. Both imperatives have resounded with enduring effect among the Jews since biblical times. Indeed, in trying to understand the survival of a people that has spent most of its life in global dispersion, I would submit that the history of its memory, largely neglected and yet to be written, may prove of some consequence.

But what were the Jews to remember, and by what means? What have been the functional dynamics of Jewish memory, and how, if at all, is the command to remember related to the writing of history? For historiography, an actual recording of historical events, is by no means the principal medium through which the collective memory of the Jewish people has been addressed or aroused. The apparent irony is not limited to the Jews alone. It is our common experience that what is remembered is not always

5

recorded and, alas for the historian, that much of what has been recorded is not necessarily remembered.

In the space of these lectures I shall not venture to treat the relations between Jewish memory and the writing of Jewish history in all their tangled configurations. Nor do I propose to attempt a history of Jewish historiography. For it is not historical writing *per se* that will concern us here, but the relation of Jews to their own past, and the place of the historian within that relationship. What I have to say is ultimately quite personal. It flows out of lingering preoccupations with the nature of my craft, but I do not presume to speak for the guild. I trust that, by the time I have done, the personal will not seem merely arbitrary. I would add only that although, as an historian of the Jews, I am concerned primarily with the Jewish past, I do not think that the issues to be raised are necessarily confined to Jewish history. Still, it may be that this history can sometimes set them into sharper relief than would otherwise be possible. And with that we may begin.

*   *   *

For those reared and educated in the modern West it is often hard to grasp the fact that a concern with history, let alone the writing of history, is not an innate endowment of human civilization. Many cultures past and present have found no particular virtue in the historical, temporal dimension, of human existence. Out of a mass of ethnographic materials from around the world anthropologists and historians of religion have gradually clarified the extent to which, in primitive societies, only mythic rather than historical time is "real," the time of primeval beginnings and paradigmatic first acts, the dream-time when the world was new, suffering unknown, and men consorted with the gods. Indeed, in such cultures the present historical moment possesses little independent value. It achieves meaning and reality only by subverting itself, when, through the repetition of a ritual or the recitation or re-enactment of a myth, historical time is periodically shattered and one can experience again, if only briefly, the true time of the origins and archetypes.[2] Nor are these vital functions of myth and ritual confined to the so-called primitives. Along with the mentality they reflect they are also shared by the great pagan religions of antiquity and beyond. In the metaphysics and epistemology of some of the most sophisticated of Far Eastern civilizations, both time and history are deprecated as illusory, and to be liberated from such illusions is a condition for true knowledge and ultimate salvation. These and similar matters are well documented in an abundant literature and need not be belabored here. Lest our discussion remain too abstract, however, let me cite one striking example in the case of India, of which a noted modern Indian scholar writes:

. . . the fact remains that except Kalhana's *Rajatarangini*, which is merely a local history of Kashmir, there is no other historical text in the whole range of Sanskrit literature which even makes a near approach to it, or may be regarded as history in the proper sense of the term. This is a very strange phenomenon, for there is hardly a branch of human knowledge or any topic of human interest which is not adequately represented in Sanskrit literature. The absence of real historical literature is therefore naturally regarded as so very unusual that even many distinguished Indians cannot bring themselves to recognize the obvious fact, and seriously entertain the belief that there were many such historical texts, but that they have all perished.[3]

Herodotus, we are told, was the "father of history" (a phrase that needs to be qualified, but I shall not pause to do so here), and until fairly recently every educated person knew that the Greeks had produced a line of great historians who could still be read with pleasure and empathy. Yet neither the Greek historians nor the civilization that nurtured them saw any ultimate or transcendent meaning to history as a whole; indeed, they never quite arrived at a concept of universal history, of history "as a whole." Herodotus wrote with the very human aspiration of—in his own words—"preserving from decay the remembrance of what men have done,

and of preventing the great and wonderful actions of the Greeks
and the barbarians from losing their due meed of glory." For
Herodotus the writing of history was first and foremost a bulwark
against the inexorable erosion of memory engendered by the
passage of time. In general, the historiography of the Greeks was
an expression of that splendid Hellenic curiosity to know and to
explore which can still draw us close to them, or else it sought
from the past moral examples or political insights. Beyond that,
history had no truths to offer, and thus it had no place in Greek
religion or philosophy. If Herodotus was the father of history, the
fathers of meaning in history were the Jews.[4]

It was ancient Israel that first assigned a decisive significance to
history and thus forged a new world-view whose essential premises
were eventually appropriated by Christianity and Islam as well.
"The heavens," in the words of the psalmist, might still "declare
the glory of the Lord," but it was human history that revealed his
will and purpose. This novel perception was not the result of
philosophical speculation, but of the peculiar nature of Israelite
faith. It emerged out of an intuitive and revolutionary understanding of God, and was refined through profoundly felt historical experiences. However it came about, in retrospect the consequences
are manifest. Suddenly, as it were, the crucial encounter between
man and the divine shifted away from the realm of nature and the
cosmos to the plane of history, conceived now in terms of divine
challenge and human response. The pagan conflict of the gods
with the forces of chaos, or with one another, was replaced by a
drama of a different and more poignant order: the paradoxical
struggle between the divine will of an omnipotent Creator and the
free will of his creature, man, in the course of history; a tense
dialectic of obedience and rebellion. The primeval dream-time
world of the archetypes, represented in the Bible only by the Para-
dise story in Genesis, was abandoned irrevocably.[5] With the departure of Adam and Eve from Eden, history begins, historical time
becomes real, and the way back is closed forever. East of Eden
hangs "the fiery ever-turning sword" to bar re-entry. Thrust reluc-

tantly into history, man in Hebrew thought comes to affirm his historical existence despite the suffering it entails, and gradually, ploddingly, he discovers that God reveals himself in the course of it. Rituals and festivals in ancient Israel are themselves no longer primarily repetitions of mythic archetypes meant to annihilate historical time. Where they evoke the past, it is not the primeval but the historical past, in which the great and critical moments of Israel's history were fulfilled. Far from attempting a flight from history, biblical religion allows itself to be saturated by it and is inconceivable apart from it.

No more dramatic evidence is needed for the dominant place of history in ancient Israel than the overriding fact that even God is known only insofar as he reveals himself "historically." Sent to bring the tidings of deliverance to the Hebrew slaves, Moses does not come in the name of the Creator of Heaven and Earth, but of the "God of the fathers," that is to say, of the God of history: "Go and assemble the elders of Israel and say to them: The Lord the God of your fathers, the God of Abraham, Isaac and Jacob has appeared to me and said: I have surely remembered you . . ." (Exod. 3:16). When God introduces himself directly to the entire people at Sinai, nothing is heard of his essence or attributes, but only: "I the Lord am your God who brought you out of the Land of Egypt, the house of bondage" (Exod. 20:2). That is sufficient. For here as elsewhere, ancient Israel knows what God is from what he has done in history.[6] And if that is so, then memory has become crucial to its faith and, ultimately, to its very existence.

Only in Israel and nowhere else is the injunction to remember felt as a religious imperative to an entire people. Its reverberations are everywhere, but they reach a crescendo in the Deuteronomic history and in the prophets. "Remember the days of old, consider the years of ages past" (Deut. 32:7). "Remember these things, O Jacob, for you, O Israel, are My servant; I have fashioned you, you are My servant; O Israel, never forget Me" (Is. 44:21). "Remember what Amalek did to you" (Deut. 25:17). "O My people, remember now what Balak king of Moab plotted against you"

(Micah 6:5). And, with a hammering insistence: "Remember
that you were a slave in Egypt. . . ."

If the command to remember is absolute, there is, nonetheless,
an almost desperate pathos about the biblical concern with memory, and a shrewd wisdom that knows how short and fickle human
memory can be. Not history, as is commonly supposed, but only
mythic time repeats itself. If history is real, then the Red Sea can
be crossed only once, and Israel cannot stand twice at Sinai, a
Hebrew counterpart, if you wish, to the wisdom of Heraclitus.[7]
Yet the covenant is to endure forever. "I make this covenant, with
its sanctions, not with you alone, but both with those who are
standing here with us this day before the Lord our God, and also
with those who are not with us here this day" (Deut. 29:13–14).
It is an outrageous claim. Surely there comes a day "when your
children will ask you in time to come, saying: What mean you by
these stones? Then you shall say to them: Because the waters of
the Jordan were cut off before the ark of the covenant of the Lord
when it passed through the Jordan" (Josh. 4:6–7). Not the stone,
but the memory transmitted by the fathers, is decisive if the memory embedded in the stone is to be conjured out of it to live again
for subsequent generations. If there can be no return to Sinai, then
what took place at Sinai must be borne along the conduits of memory to those who were not there that day.

The biblical appeal to remember thus has little to do with
curiosity about the past. Israel is told only that it must be a kingdom of priests and a holy people; nowhere is it suggested that it
become a nation of historians. Memory is, by its nature, selective,
and the demand that Israel remember is no exception. Burckhardt's
dictum that all ages are equally close to God may please us, but
such a notion remains alien to biblical thought. There the fact that
history has meaning does not mean that everything that happened
in history is meaningful or worthy of recollection. Of Manasseh
of Judah, a powerful king who reigned for fifty-five years in Jerusalem, we hear only that "he did what was evil in the sight of the
Lord" (II Kings 21:2), and only the details of that evil are

conveyed to us. Not only is Israel under no obligation whatever to remember the entire past, but its principle of selection is unique unto itself. It is above all God's acts of intervention in history, and man's responses to them, be they positive or negative, that must be recalled. Nor is the invocation of memory actuated by the normal and praiseworthy desire to preserve heroic national deeds from oblivion. Ironically, many of the biblical narratives seem almost calculated to deflate the national ̄pride. For the real danger is not so much that what happened in the past will be forgotten, as the more crucial aspect of *how* it happened. "And it shall be, when the Lord your God shall bring you into the land which he swore unto your fathers, to Abraham, to Isaac, and to Jacob, to give you great and goodly cities, which you did not build, and houses full of all good things, which you did not fill, and cisterns hewn out, which you did not hew, vineyards and olive-trees which you did not plant, and you shall eat and be satisfied—*then beware lest you forget the Lord who brought you forth out of the land of Egypt, out of the house of bondage*" (Deut. 6:10–12; cf. 8:11–18).

Memory flowed, above all, through two channels: ritual and recital. Even while fully preserving their organic links to the natural cycles of the agricultural year (spring and first fruits), the great pilgrimage festivals of Passover and Tabernacles were transformed into commemorations of the Exodus from Egypt and the sojourn in the wilderness. (Similarly, the biblical Feast of Weeks would become, sometime in the period of the Second Temple, a commemoration of the giving of the Law at Sinai.) Oral poetry preceded and sometimes accompanied the prose of the chroniclers. For the Hebrew reader even now such survivals as the Song of the Sea (Exod. 15:1–18) or the Song of Deborah (Judges 5) seem possessed of a curious power to evoke, through the sheer force of their archaic rhythms and images, distant but strangely moving intimations of an experience of primal events whose factual details are perhaps irrevocably lost.

A superlative example of the interplay of ritual and recital in the service of memory is the ceremony of the first fruits ordained in Deuteronomy 26, where the celebrant, an ordinary Israelite bringing his fruits to the sanctuary, must make the following declaration:

A wandering Aramean was my father, and he went down into Egypt, and sojourned there, few in number; and he became there a nation, great, mighty, and populous. And the Egyptians dealt ill with us, and afflicted us, and laid upon us hard bondage. And we cried unto the Lord, the God of our fathers, and the Lord heard our voice, and saw our affliction, and our toil, and our oppression. And the Lord brought us forth out of Egypt with a mighty hand, and with an outstretched arm, and with great terribleness, and with signs, and with wonders. And He has brought us into this place, and has given us this land, a land flowing with milk and honey . . . (Deut. 25:5–9).[8]

This is capsule history at its best. The essentials to be remembered are all here, in a ritualized formula. Compressed within it are what we might paraphrase as the patriarchal origins in Mesopotamia, the emergence of the Hebrew nation in the midst of history rather than in mythic pre-history, slavery in Egypt and liberation therefrom, the climactic acquisition of the Land of Israel, and throughout—the acknowledgment of God as lord of history.

Yet although the continuity of memory could be sustained by such means, and while fundamental biblical conceptions of history were forged, not by historians, but by priests and prophets, the need to remember overflowed inevitably into actual historical narrative as well. In the process, and within that varied Hebrew literature spanning a millennium which we laconically call "the Bible," a succession of anonymous authors created the most distinguished corpus of historical writing in the ancient Near East.

It was an astonishing achievement by any standard applicable to ancient historiography, all the more so when we bear in mind some of its own presuppositions. With God as the true hero of history one wonders at the very human scale of the historical narratives themselves. Long familiarity should not make us indifferent to such qualities. There was no compelling *a priori* reason why the biblical historians should not have been content to produce an episodic account of divine miracles and little else. Yet if biblical history has, at its core, a recital of the acts of God, its accounts are filled predominantly with the actions of men and women and the deeds of Israel and the nations. Granted that historical writing in ancient Israel had its roots in the belief that history was a theophany and that events were ultimately to be interpreted in light of this faith. The result was, not theology, but history on an unprecedented scale.

Another surprising feature in most of biblical historiography is its concreteness. Where we might have expected a re-telling of Israel's past that would continually sacrifice fact to legend and specific detail to preconceived patterns, we find instead a firm anchorage in historical realities. The events and characteristics of one age are seldom blurred with those of another. Discrepancies between the hopes of an early generation and the situation encountered by a later one are not erased. (Compare, for example, the promised boundaries of the Land of Israel with those of the territories actually conquered in Canaan.)[9] Historical figures emerge not merely as types, but as full-fledged individuals. Chronology, by and large, is respected. There is a genuine sense of the flow of historical time and of the changes that occur within it. Abraham is not represented as observing the laws of Moses. The editors who periodically redacted the sources at their disposal did not level them out completely. Two essentially conflicting accounts of the origins of Israelite monarchy lie side by side to this day in the Book of Samuel.

That biblical historiography is not "factual" in the modern sense is too self-evident to require extensive comment. By the same token, however, its poetic or legendary elements are not "fictions" in the modern sense either. For a people in ancient times these were legitimate and sometimes inevitable modes of historical perception and interpretation.[10] But biblical historiography is hardly uniform in these respects. The historical narratives that span the ages from the beginnings of mankind to the conquest of

Canaan are necessarily more legendary, the accounts of the monarchy much less so, and even within each segment there are marked variations of degree. This is only to be expected. The historical texts of the Bible, written by different authors at different times, were often also the end products of a long process of transmission of earlier documents and traditions.

I cannot pause here to discuss the stages by which either biblical interpretations of history or the actual writing of history evolved. In terms of our larger concerns, such an atomistic discussion might even prove misleading. By the second century B.C.E. the corpus of biblical writings was already complete, and its subsequent impact upon Jewry was in its totality. Post-biblical Judaism did not inherit a series of separate historical sources and documents, but what it regarded as a sacred and organic whole. Read through from Genesis through Chronicles it offered not only a repository of law, wisdom, and faith, but a coherent narrative that claimed to embrace the whole of history from the creation of the world to the fifth century B.C.E., and, in the prophetic books, a profound interpretation of that history as well. With the Book of Daniel, the last of the biblical books in point of actual composition, an apocalyptic exposition of world history was incorporated as well, which would exercise its own particular fascination in ages to come.

Obviously much more could still be said about the place and function of history in ancient Israel that I have chosen to ignore. But if we really seek to understand what happened later, then we may already have touched on something that can prove of considerable help, and should therefore be reformulated explicitly. We have learned, in effect, that meaning in history, memory of the past, and the writing of history are by no means to be equated. In the Bible, to be sure, the three elements are linked, they overlap at critical points, and, in general, they are held together in a web of delicate and reciprocal relationships. In post-biblical Judaism, as we shall see, they pull asunder. Even in the Bible, however, historiography is but one expression of the awareness that history is meaningful and of the need to remember, and neither meaning nor memory ultimately depends upon it. The meaning of history is explored more directly and more deeply in the prophets than in the actual historical narratives;[11] the collective memory is transmitted more actively through ritual than through chronicle. Conversely, in Israel as in Greece, historiography could be propelled by other needs and considerations. There were other, more mundane, genres of historical writing, apparently quite unrelated to the quest for transcendent meanings.[12] Of the same Manasseh who did evil in the sight of the Lord we read, as we do of other monarchs, that the rest of his acts are written "in the books of the chronicles of the kings of Judah." Significantly perhaps, those royal chronicles are long lost to us.

If Joshua, Samuel, Kings, and the other historical books of the Bible were destined to survive, that is because something quite extraordinary happened to them. They had become part of an authoritative anthology of sacred writings whose final canonization took place at Yabneh in Palestine around the year 100 C.E., some thirty years after the destruction of the Second Temple by the Romans. With the sealing of the biblical canon by the rabbis at Yabneh, the biblical historical books and narratives were endowed with an immortality to which no subsequent historian could ever aspire and that was denied to certain historical works that already existed. The Jewish historiography of the Hellenistic period, even such works as the first three books of Maccabees, fell by the wayside, some of it to be preserved by the Christian church, but unavailable to the Jews themselves until modern times.[13]

That which was included in the biblical canon had, so to speak, a constantly renewable lease on life, and we must try to savor some of what this has meant. For the first time the history of a people became part of its sacred scripture. The Pentateuchal narratives, which brought the historical record up to the eve of the conquest of Canaan, together with the weekly lesson from the prophets, were read aloud in the synagogue from beginning to end. The public reading was completed triennially in Palestine, annually in Babylonia (as is the custom today), and immediately the reading would begin again.[14] Every generation of scribes would copy and transmit the historical texts with the reverent care that only the sacred can command. An unbroken chain of scholars would arise later to explicate what had been recorded long ago in a constantly receding past. With the gradual democratization of Jewish learning, both the recitals of ancient chroniclers and the interpretations of prophets long dead would become the patrimony, not of a minority, but of the people at large.

To many, therefore, it has seemed all the more remarkable that after the close of the biblical canon the Jews virtually stopped writing history. Josephus Flavius marks the watershed. Writing in a not-uncomfortable Roman exile after the destruction of the Second Temple, sometime between 75 and 79 C.E. Josephus published his account of the *Jewish War* against Rome and then went on to an elaborate summation of the history of his people in the *Jewish Antiquities*. The latter work was published in 93/94, that is, less than a decade before the rabbis held their council at Yabneh. By coincidence the two events were almost contemporaneous. Yet in retrospect we know that within Jewry the future belonged to the rabbis, not to Josephus. Not only did his works not survive among the Jews, it would be almost fifteen centuries before another Jew would actually call himself an historian.[15] It is as though, abruptly, the impulse to historiography had ceased.

Certainly, when we turn from the Bible to classical rabbinic literature, be it Talmud or Midrash, we seem to find ourselves on different and unfamiliar terrain as far as history is concerned. Where the Bible, with austere restraint, had said little or nothing of God prior to the creation of the world we know, here we encounter the periodic creation and destruction of worlds before our own.[16] Ancient Near Eastern mythological motifs of divine victories over primeval monsters, of which only faint and vestigial traces are preserved in the Bible, suddenly reassert themselves more vividly and elaborately than before.[17] To be sure, all the historical events and personalities of the Bible are present in rabbinic aggadah; indeed, much more is told about them by the rabbis than in the Bible itself. Guided often by an uncanny eye for gaps, problems, and nuances, the rabbis amplified the biblical narratives with remarkable sensitivity. The wide range of biblically based rabbinic aggadah has enchanted poets and intrigued anthropologists and folklorists, theologians and philosophers. Even a modern critical scholar of the Bible will often find that behind a particular midrash there lies a genuine issue in the biblical text, whether linguistic or substantive, of which he was himself previously unaware. But the fascination and importance of rabbinic literature are not at issue here. It is the historian within all of us that balks, and we recognize some of the reasons for our frustration. Unlike the biblical writers the rabbis seem to play with Time as though with an accordion, expanding and collapsing it at will. Where historical specificity is a hallmark of the biblical narratives, here that acute biblical sense of time and place often gives way to rampant and seemingly unselfconscious anachronism. In the world of aggadah Adam can instruct his son Seth in the Torah, Shem and Eber establish a house of study, the patriarchs institute the three daily prayer-services of the normative Jewish liturgy, Og King of Bashan is present at Isaac's circumcision, and Noah prophesies the translation of the Bible into Greek.

Of course there is something rather compelling about that large portion of the rabbinic universe in which ordinary barriers of time can be ignored and all the ages placed in an ever-fluid dialogue with one another. Clearly, however, something else that we would consider vital has also been lost in the course of this metamorphosis, and we need not look far to know what it is. The history of the biblical period is present in the Bible itself. Admittedly, the reconstruction of that history through modern critical scholarship, buttressed by archaeology and the recovery of ancient Near Eastern languages and literatures, now offers a more contextual understanding than was ever possible before, and can sometimes diverge sharply from the accounts and interpretations of the biblical writers themselves. But at least the biblical record is sufficiently historical to serve the modern scholar as a constant point of departure and reference for his researches. By contrast, no such reconstruction would be possible if it had to depend, not on the Bible, but on the rabbinic sources that "retell" biblical history. This would be so even if everything the rabbis told were linked together and arranged into one continuous narrative parallel to the biblical sequence, as in Ginzberg's prodigious *Legends of the Jews*.[18]

More sobering and important is the fact that the history of the Talmudic period itself cannot be elicited from its own vast literature. Historical events of the first order are either not recorded at all, or else they are mentioned in so legendary or fragmentary a way as often to preclude even an elementary retrieval of what occurred.[19]

All this raises two distinct issues. One concerns what the rabbis actually accomplished, the other, what they did not undertake to do.

It is both unfair and misleading to burden the transmutations of biblical personalities and events in rabbinic aggadah with a demand for historicity irrelevant to their nature and purpose. Classical rabbinic literature was never intended as historiography, even in the biblical, let alone the modern, sense, and it cannot be understood through canons of criticism appropriate to history alone. Anachronism, for example, may be a serious flaw in historical writing; it is a legitimate feature of other, non-historical genres. There is no more point in asking of rabbinic aggadah that it hew closely to the biblical historical record than to try to divest the biblical figures in Renaissance paintings of their Florentine costumes, or to carp at MacLeish for presenting Job as "J. B." to a twentieth-century audience. The rabbis did not set out to write a history of the biblical period; they already possessed that. Instead, they were engrossed in an ongoing exploration of the meaning of the history bequeathed to them, striving to interpret it in living terms for their own and later generations.[20] Just as, in their exposition of biblical law, they explained the *lex talionis* as a principle of monetary compensation rather than a more "historical" eye-for-an-eye, so they were not content with merely historical patriarchs and kings endowed with the obsolete traits of a dead past. This does not mean necesssarily that they were bereft of all sense of historical perspective. They were certainly not naive. Without having a term for it they occasionally showed themselves quite capable of recognizing an anachronism for what it was,[21] but they were also able somehow to sustain and reconcile historical contradictions that we, for that very reason, would find intolerable. I know of no more telling instance of the fusion of both tendencies than what is revealed in this remarkable Talmudic aggadah:

Rabbi Judah said in the name of Rab: When Moses ascended on high [to receive the Torah] he found the Holy One, blessed be He, engaged in affixing *taggin* [crown-like flourishes] to the letters. Moses said: "Lord of the Universe, who stays Thy hand?" [i.e., is there anything lacking in the Torah so that these ornaments are necessary?] He replied: "There will arise a man at the end of many generations, Akiba ben Joseph by name, who will expound, upon each tittle, heaps and heaps of laws." "Lord of the Universe," said Moses, "permit me to see him." He replied: "Turn thee round."
Moses went [into the academy of Rabbi Akiba] and sat down behind eight rows [of Akiba's disciples]. *Not being able to follow their arguments he was ill at ease*, but when they came to a certain subject and the disciples said to the master "Whence do you know it?" and the latter replied, "*It is a law given to Moses at Sinai*," he was comforted.[22]

That the whole of the Law, not only the written (*torah she-biketab*), but also the "oral" (*torah she-be'al peh*), had already been revealed to Moses at Sinai, was an axiom of rabbinic belief;[23] nevertheless, were Moses transported to a second-century classroom, he would hardly understand the legal discussions. In the world of aggadah both propositions can coexist in a meaningful equilibrium without appearing anomalous or illogical. Similarly, elements of biblical history can be telescoped into legendary dimensions with no intimation that either the past or the Bible has been compromised thereby. The historical record remains intact within an inviolate biblical text to which, in a perpetual oscillation, the aggadic imagination must always return before its next flight. Meanwhile, however, any event can be retold and reinterpreted, sometimes simultaneously, in several different ways. Patently, by that very token the assumptions and hermeneutics of the rabbis were often antithetical to those of the historian, and generally remote from ours even when we are not historians.[24] But they were appropriate to their particular quest, which was equally far removed from our own.

A problem of a very different sort is posed by the meager attention accorded in rabbinic literature to post-biblical events. While we can accept the aggadic transfigurations of biblical history as forms of commentary and interpretation, we may still ask, tentatively at least, why the rabbis did not see fit to take up where biblical history broke off.

For the fact is that the rabbis neither wrote post-biblical history nor made any special effort to preserve what they may have known of the course of historical events in the ages immediately preceding them or in their own time. The two solitary works frequently trotted out to demonstrate the contrary need not detain us long. *Megillat Ta'anit*, the so-called "Scroll of Fasting," is not an attempt at historiography but a terse calendar of thirty-five half-holidays originating in the Hasmonean period and commemorating various historical events, most of them connected with the Maccabean wars.[25] Such a calendar was preserved purely for its practical ritual consequences, since on the days it enumerates one was not to declare a public fast (hence the curious title) nor mourn the dead. Significantly, it notes the day of the month on which the events occurred, but not the year. At best only the other work, the *Seder 'Olam* ("Order of the World")[26] attributed to the second-century Palestinian rabbi Jose ben Halafta, may qualify as a rudimentary sort of historical recording, but even then it remains the exception that confirms the rule. It is, in essence, a dry chronology of persons and events from Adam until Alexander the Great that hardly pauses for breath while relentlessly listing its succession of names and years. Apart from this, the attempts by some modern scholars to find traces of historiography in the Talmudic period merely reflect a misplaced projection of their own concerns upon a reluctant past.[27]

Does this signify, as is so often alleged, that the rabbis were no longer interested in history? Surely not. Prophecy had ceased, but the rabbis regarded themselves as heirs to the prophets, and this was proper, for they had thoroughly assimilated the prophetic world-view and made it their own.[28] For them history was no less meaningful, their God no less the ultimate arbiter of historical destinies, their messianic hope no less fervent and absolute. But where the prophets themselves had been attuned to the interpretation of contemporary historical events, the rabbis are relatively silent about the events of their own time. In Talmudic and midrashic literature there are many interpretations of the meaning of history, but little desire to record current events. It is this characteristic concern for the larger configurations of history, coupled with indifference to its concrete particulars, that deserves some explanation.

We will state it as simply as possible. If the rabbis, wise men who had inherited a powerful historical tradition, were no longer interested in mundane history, this indicates nothing more than that they felt no need to cultivate it. Perhaps they already knew of history what they needed to know. Perhaps they were even wary of it.

For the rabbis the Bible was not only a repository of past history, but a revealed pattern of the whole of history, and they had learned their scriptures well. They knew that history has a purpose, the establishment of the kingdom of God on earth, and that the Jewish people has a central role to play in the process. They were convinced that the covenant between God and Israel was eternal, though the Jews had often rebelled and suffered the consequences. Above all, they had learned from the Bible that the true pulse of history often beat beneath its manifest surfaces, an invisible history that was more real than what the world, deceived by the more strident outward rhythms of power, could recognize. Assyria had been the instrument of divine wrath against Israel, even though Assyria had not realized it at the time. Jerusalem had fallen to Nebuchadnezzar, not because of Babylonian might, but because of Jerusalem's transgressions, and because God had allowed it to fall. Over against the triumphalism which was the conventional historical wisdom of the nations there loomed, as though in silent rebuke, the figure of the Suffering Servant of Isaiah 53.

Ironically, the very absence of historical writing among the rabbis may itself have been due in good measure to their total and unqualified absorption of the biblical interpretation of history. In its ensemble the biblical record seemed capable of illuminating every further historical contingency. No fundamentally new conception of history had to be forged in order to accommodate Rome, nor, for that matter, any of the other world empires that would arise subsequently. The catastrophe of the year 70 C.E. was due, like that of 586 B.C.E., to sin, although the rabbis were well aware that the nature of the sin had changed and was no longer one of idolatry.[29] The Roman triumph, like that of the earlier empires, would not endure forever:

Rabbi Nahman opened his discourse with the text, *Therefore fear thou not, O Jacob My servant* (Jer. 30:10). This speaks of Jacob himself, of whom it is written, *And he dreamed, and behold, a ladder set up on the earth . . . and behold the angels of God ascending and descending on it* (Gen. 28:12). These angels, explained Rabbi Samuel ben Nahman, were the guardian Princes of the nations of the world. For Rabbi Samuel ben Nahman said: This verse teaches us that the Holy One, blessed be He, showed our father Jacob the Prince of Babylon ascending seventy rungs of the ladder, the Prince of Media fifty-two rungs, the Prince of Greece one hundred and eighty, while the Prince of Edom [i.e., Rome] ascended till Jacob did not know how many rungs. Thereupon our father Jacob was afraid. He thought: Is it possible that this one will never be brought down? Said the Holy One, blessed be He, to him: *"Fear thou not, O Jacob My servant. Even if he ascend and sit down by Me, I will bring him down from there."*

Hence it is written, *Though thou make thy nest as high as the eagle,*
and though thou set it among the stars, I will bring thee down from
thence (Obad. 1:4).[30]

Destruction and redemption were dialectically linked. We are
told: "On the day the Temple was destroyed the Messiah was
born." Should you then, want to know where he is, here is one
version:

Rabbi Joshua ben Levi met Elijah standing by the entrance to the
cave of Rabbi Simon bar Yohai . . . He asked him: "When will the
Messiah come?"—He replied: "Go and ask him."—"And where is he
sitting?"—"At the entrance to the city of Rome."—"And by what
sign may he be recognized?"—"He is sitting among the poor lepers.
But whereas they untie their bandages all at once and tie them back
together, he unties and ties each separately, thinking: 'Perhaps I will
be summoned. Let me not be delayed.' "

Rabbi Joshua went to the Messiah and said to him: "Peace upon
you, my master and teacher."—"Peace upon you, son of Levi," he
replied.—He asked: "When will you come, master?"—He answered:
"Today!"

Rabbi Joshua returned to Elijah. The latter asked him: "What did
he say to you?" . . . He replied: "He lied to me, for he said that he
would come today, yet he has not come."—Elijah answered: "This is
what he said to you—*Today, if ye would but hearken to His voice* (Ps.
95:7)."[31]

If, in these potent images, the history of the world empires is a
Jacob's Ladder and the messiah sits unnoticed at the gates of Rome
ready, sooner or later, to bring about her downfall, then the affairs
of Rome may well appear inconsequential and ordinary historical
knowledge superfluous. Whether, as R. Joshua found, the messianic advent is contingent upon Jewish repentance and obedience
to God, or even if, as others claimed, it will take place indepen-
dently, at the inscrutable initiative of the divine will, the question
of what to do in the interim remained. Here the rabbis were

unanimous. In the interval between destruction and redemption
the primary Jewish task was to respond finally and fully to the
biblical challenge of becoming a holy people. And for them that
meant the study and fulfillment of the written and oral law, the
establishment of a Jewish society based fully on its precepts and
ideals, and, where the future was concerned, trust, patience, and
prayer.

Compared to these firm foundations contemporary history must
have seemed a realm of shifting sands. The biblical past was
known, the messianic future assured; the in-between-time was
obscure. Then as now, history did not validate itself and reveal
its meaning imminently. In the biblical period the meaning of
specific historical events had been laid bare by the inner eye of
prophecy, but that was no longer possible. If the rabbis were
successors to the prophets they did not themselves lay claim to
prophecy. The comings and goings of Roman procurators, the
dynastic affairs of Roman emperors, the wars and conquests of
Parthians and Sassanians, seemed to yield no new or useful insights
beyond what was already known. Even the convolutions of the
Hasmonean dynasty or the intrigues of Herodians—Jewish history
after all—revealed nothing relevant and were largely ignored.[32]

Only messianic activism still had the capacity to revive and rivet
attention on current historical events and even lead to direct action
on the historical plane, but attempts to "hasten the end" became
discredited out of bitter experience. Three tremendous uprisings
against Rome, all with eschatological overtones, had ended in
disaster and disillusion. In the second century, no less an authority
than Rabbi Akiba could hail Bar Kochba, the military leader of
the revolt of 132, as the Messiah. Thereafter the tendency to dis-
courage and combat messianic activism in any form, already evident earlier, became a dominant characteristic of responsible rabbinic leadership for ages to come.[33] The faith of rabbinic Judaism
in the coming of the Messiah remained unshaken; the time of his
coming was left to heaven alone. R. Samuel bar Nahmani declared: "Blasted be those who calculate the end, for they say that

since the time has arrived and he has not come, he will never come. Rather—wait for him, as it is written: Though he tarry, wait for him. . . ."[34] The scrutiny of outward historical events for signs that the end of time was approaching remained largely the province of apocalyptic visionaries who continued to surface periodically throughout the centuries.

As for the sages themselves—they salvaged what they felt to be relevant to them, and that meant, in effect, what was relevant to the ongoing religious and communal (hence also the "national") life of the Jewish people. They did not preserve the political history of the Hasmoneans, but took note of the conflict between the Pharisees and Alexander Jannaeus.[35] They did not incorporate a consecutive history of the period of the Second Temple or its destruction, but they carefully wrote down the details of the Temple service, convinced of its eventual restoration.[36] They betrayed scant interest in the history of Rome, but they would not forget the persecution under the emperor Hadrian and the martyrdom of the scholars.[37] True, they also ignored the battles of the Maccabees in favor of the cruse of oil that burned for eight days, but their recognition of this particular miracle should not be passed over lightly. Hanukkah alone, be it noted, was a post-biblical Jewish holiday, and the miracle, unlike others, did not have behind it the weight of biblical authority. The very acceptance of such a miracle was therefore a reaffirmation of faith in the continuing intervention of God in history. Indeed, we may well ponder the audacity with which the rabbis fixed the formal Hanukkah benediction as: "Blessed be Thou O Lord our God . . . *who has commanded us* to kindle the Hanukkah light."[38]

I suspect, of course, that many moderns would rather have the Maccabees than the miracle. If so, that is assuredly a modern problem, and not that of the rabbis. They obviously felt they had all the history they required, and it will help us neither to applaud nor to deplore this. To continue to ask why they did not write post-biblical history or, as we shall yet see, why medieval Jews wrote so little, is somewhat reminiscent of those "educated" Indians who, westernized under the benevolent auspices of the British Raj, are embarassed by the absence of historiography in their own tradition and cannot reconcile themselves to it.

We, I think, can afford to be less troubled. We can acknowledge serenely that in rabbinic Judaism, which was to permeate Jewish life the world over, historiography came to a long halt even while belief in the meaning of history remained. We can freely concede, moreover, that much in the rabbinic (and even the biblical) heritage inculcated patterns and habits of thought in later generations that were, from a modern point of view, if not anti-historical, then at least ahistorical. Yet these factors did not inhibit the transmission of a vital Jewish past from one generation to the next, and Judaism neither lost its link to history nor its fundamentally historical orientation. The difficulty in grasping this apparent incongruity lies in a poverty of language that forces us, *faute de mieux*, to apply the term "history" both to the sort of past with which we are concerned, and to that of Jewish tradition.

Some of the differences have already surfaced, others will become clearer as we go along, for what we have discussed thus far is only preparatory to what remains to be unravelled of our larger theme. The next lecture will focus on specific instances of how Jewish memory functioned in the Middle Ages. We will go on from there to examine the brief but significant renaissance of Jewish historical writing in the sixteenth century. Finally, we will marshal our accumulated resources to probe a phenomenon that is still very much with us—the unprecedented explosion of Jewish historiography in modern times.

2

THE MIDDLE AGES

Vessels and Vehicles of Jewish Memory

A parable: To what is this like? To a man who was travel-
ling on the road when he encountered a wolf and escaped
from it, and he went along relating the affair of the wolf. He
then encountered a lion and escaped from it, and went along
relating the affair of the lion. He then encountered a snake
and escaped from it, whereupon he forgot the two previous
incidents and went along relating the affair of the snake. So
with Israel. The latter troubles make them forget the earlier
ones.

—TB *Berakhot* 13a

He who answered Abraham our father at Mount Moriah,
    He shall answer us, and all the holy communities,
    and all those immersed in sorrow and affliction,
    and all who are bound in prison under kings and princes ...
He who answered Moses at the Red Sea,
    He shall answer us ...
He who answered Joshua at Gilgal,
    He shall answer us ...
He who answered Samuel at Mizpah,
    He shall answer us ...
He who answered Elijah on Mount Carmel,
    He shall answer us ...
He who answered Jonah in the belly of the fish,
    He shall answer us ...
He who answered David and Solomon in Jerusalem,
    He shall answer us ...

                —From the liturgy for a public fast
                 (based on Mishnah *Ta'anit* 2:4)

W̶e find in almost all branches of Jewish literature in the Middle Ages a wealth of thought on the position of the Jewish people in history, of ideas of Jewish history, of often profound and sometimes daring reflections on exile and redemption, but comparatively little interest in recording the on-going historical experience of the Jews. There is much on the meaning of Jewish history; there is little historiography. Interpretations of history, whether explicit or veiled, can be encountered in works of philosophy, homiletics, biblical exegesis, law, mysticism, most often without a single mention of actual historical events or personalities, and with no attempt to relate to them. In light of our prior discussion, this should come as no particular surprise.

Some historical works were certainly written by medieval Jews, but they were few in number. In their ensemble they simply did not constitute a phenomenon of the sort to be found among other peoples in whose midst Jews lived and created. Having been interrupted in the Talmudic period, no tradition of historical writing re-emerged, no genre with accepted conventions or continuity. Those historical works that were written appeared only sporadically. By and large the distance between them in time and space is significant, the periods of silence long.[1]

Only in one well-defined area can one speak of a genre, and that is the literature of the so-called "chain of tradition" of the Oral Law (*shalshelet ha-qabbalah*). Such works surveyed chronologically the transmission of rabbinic law and doctrine by recording the sequence of luminaries who were its bearers through the ages. The purpose was to establish and demonstrate an unbroken succession of teaching and authority from the Bible, through the Talmud, and often up to the time of the author himself.[2] Only this type of historiography achieved legitimacy and found a home within medieval Judaism, and here alone can one discern a certain continuity of effort, from the anonymous "Order of Mishnaic and

Amoraic Sages" (*Seder Tanna'im va-'Amora'im*) in the ninth
century to Yehiel Heilprin's "Order of the Generations" (*Seder
ha-dorot*) in the eighteenth. Yet for all the variations they exhibit,
and despite their significance as historical source material for us
today, the many compositions of this type did not come into being
out of a desire to write or interpret the history of the Jewish people. Their chief impulses lay elsewhere—in the need to refute
those heretics from within and adversaries from without who denied the validity of the Oral Law, in the practical need to determine
points of jurisprudence according to earlier or later authorities,
and perhaps also in a natural curiosity about the progress of rabbinic scholarship. Biographical details concerning the rabbis who
were the links in the chain of tradition are generally scanty at best,
and historical events, where they are mentioned, pop up almost
arbitrarily.

I suspect that medieval Jews often knew more history than they
chose or cared to record, and there is indirect evidence that such
was indeed the case. For example, *Iggeret Rab Sherira Gaon*, the
famous "Epistle of Sherira," head of the Babylonian academy at
Pumpeditha in the tenth century, was not composed out of an
inner need of the author, but in answer to a question sent to him
from Qairouan in North Africa as to how the corpus of Talmudic
literature came into being.[3] Sherira's responsum, which also incorporated a history of the Geonic period for which it is still our
primary source, would not have been written had it not been for
the query of the men of Qairouan. Similarly, Maimonides' "Epistle
to Yemen" (*'Iggeret Teman*) contains a brief history of four
Jewish messianic movements.[4] Were it not for the fact that a contemporary messiah had arisen in Yemen, and that in the ensuing
crisis Maimonides was asked by the Yemenite Jews to give his
opinion and advice, we would have no way of knowing that this
historical information was even available to him.

No doubt the lack of concern for historical writing on the part
of medieval Jews may be attributed in some measure to the impact
of Talmudic Judaism, the substructure for all of medieval Jewish

life and creativity. But while the ahistorical character of rabbinic thinking may have played a role in this, the mere fact that the rabbis of the Talmud had written no historical works themselves cannot quite explain what happened in later generations. Medieval Jewry created scintillating works in a number of fields that had never been cultivated before. Stimulated by close contact with Arabic culture Jews blazed new paths in philosophy, science, linguistics, secular and metrical Hebrew poetry, none of which had precedents in the Talmudic period. Only in historiography, a field in which Islamic civilization excelled and forged an important tradition, did a similar interaction fail to take place. Deeply affected by Muslim philosophy, Maimonides in the twelfth century expressed only contempt for Muslim historical works and, as is well known, considered the reading of profane history a "waste of time."[5]

The absence of a Jewish historiography was not entirely unnoticed. A generation or so before Maimonides the Spanish-Hebrew poet Moses Ibn Ezra had complained of Jewish "indolence" and even "sin" in the neglect by prior generations of both the Hebrew language and the writing of history:

. . . and they did not succeed to polish their language, to write their chronicles, and to remember their histories and traditions. It would have been fitting that they should not have ignored and despised such matters. Behold . . . all the other nations have exerted themselves to write their histories and to excel in them. . . .[6]

Yet while the neglect of the Hebrew language had already been more than rectified by the linguistic and poetic achievements of the Golden Age of Spanish Jewry, virtually nothing had changed with regard to the writing of history. Indeed, Ibn Ezra seems to have been the only one to express any concern about it. No one else was to voice a similar complaint at least until the beginning of the sixteenth century when Solomon Ibn Verga, who had grown up in Christian Spain, concluded the third chapter of his *Shebet Yehudah* with these words:

Thus is it found in the chronicles of the Kings of Persia which were brought to the King of Spain, according to the custom of the Christians, for they seek to know the things that happened of old in order to take counsel from them, and this because of their distinction and enlightenment.[7]

Significantly, for Ibn Verga it is a *Christian* custom to read historical chronicles, and here there is a note of envy that is at the same time an implicit criticism of his fellow Jews. I must emphasize, however, that I have cited both Ibn Ezra and Ibn Verga in order to establish a fact, and not because I share their judgment of it. I do not happen to be among those who, even now, would fault medieval Jewry for writing relatively little history. Far from indicating a gap or flaw in their civilization, it may well reflect a self-sufficiency that ours no longer possesses.

Nevertheless, some historical writings were produced[8] in addition to those works dealing directly with the chain of tradition, and these reveal a dominant and striking characteristic: where historical events are concerned they dwell either upon the distant, ancient past, up to the destruction of the Second Temple, or else they describe something in the most recent past, be it the latest persecution or the latest deliverance. There is little or no interest in what occurred during the long centuries between.

We should therefore distinguish between various "pasts" and not be misled into thinking that medieval Jews felt the entire past as such to be of no consequence for the present. The relevant past, however, other than that which may have been experienced directly and personally, was clearly the remote past. What had happened long ago had determined what had occurred since, and even provided the fundamental explanations for what was still transpiring.

With this in mind we can perhaps understand why it was that one book—the Hebrew history of the Second Temple period known as *Yosippon*[9]—loomed in the eyes of medieval Jewry as the single most important post-biblical chronicle. Apart from the Bible itself this was the only available work that offered a detailed narrative of ancient events in the fateful period whose repercussions were felt to extend to all subsequent generations. When, in the thirteenth century, Judah Mosconi enumerated the many virtues of the book, he wrote: "For we can read in it the deeds of our ancestors because of whose sins the city [of Jerusalem] was destroyed . . . *and they ate the sour grapes, but our teeth are set on edge.*"[10] And when, in the generation of the Spanish and Portuguese exiles, Tam Ibn Yahia sponsored a new edition of *Yosippon* published in Constantinople in 1510, he declared in his introduction:

And I, in the midst of the exile, wallowing in the blood of the upheavals that are overtaking my people and nation, was roused to be among those who have helped to print this book, for this is the one that has laid bare the source of the misfortunes of the House of Judah.[11]

Moreover, the book had the good fortune to be accepted universally as an original work written by Josephus Flavius himself in the aftermath of the fall of the Second Temple. This, it was assumed, was the Hebrew account that Josephus had written for internal Jewish consumption. Thereby *Yosippon* acquired a halo of authority among Jews that was bestowed upon no other medieval historical work, and that would have been denied to it altogether had it been suspected that this was the work of a Jew who probably lived in Southern Italy, not in the first century, but in the tenth.[12] Much of the attitude to *Yosippon* in particular and, by contrast, to historiography in general, is expressed in the following statement by Tam Ibn Yahia:

Although it is characteristic of historical works to exaggerate things that never were, to add to them, to invent things that never existed, nevertheless this book [*Yosippon*], although it is part of the same genre, is completely distinct from them, and it is the difference between truth and falsehood. For all the words of this book are righteousness and truth, and there is no wrong within it. And the mark of all this is that of all the books written after the Holy Scriptures this is [chronologically] the closest to prophecy, having been written before the Mishnah and the Talmud.[13]

More is involved here than the mere prestige of antiquity, for this passage is only one reflection of an entire mentality that expresses itself in many other ways. On the whole, medieval Jewish chronicles tend to assimilate events to old and established conceptual frameworks. Persecution and suffering are, after all, the result of the condition of being in exile, and exile itself is the bitter fruit of ancient sins. It is important to realize that there is also no real desire to find novelty in passing events. Quite to the contrary, there is a pronounced tendency to subsume even major new events to familiar archetypes, for even the most terrible events are somehow less terrifying when viewed within old patterns rather than in their bewildering specificity. Thus the latest oppressor is Haman, and the court-Jew who tries to avoid disaster is Mordecai. Christendom is "Edom" or "Esau," and Islam is "Ishmael." Geographical names are blithely lifted from the Bible and affixed to places the Bible never knew, and so Spain is "Sefarad," France is "Zarefat," Germany is "Ashkenaz."[14] The essential contours of the relations between Jews and gentiles have been delineated long ago in rabbinic aggadah, and there is little or no interest in the history of contemporary gentile nations.

In periods of acute messianic tension there may be a sudden and intense burst of interest in contemporary global events, but even here the slots, so to speak, were prepared and waiting. The now venerable tradition that four successive world-empires would precede the messianic era, first announced in the Book of Daniel and elaborated in midrashic literature, was particularly prominent whenever Jewish apocalyptic thinking rose to the surface. Invariably, it proved sufficiently elastic to accommodate every new empire into the final slot, whether by dropping one of the old ones from the sequence, or by homologizing two together and regarding them as one. A similar function was served by the allied and equally strong tradition that the messianic advent must be preceded by a final conflict between the world powers known symbolically as Gog and Magog. Candidates for these enigmatic roles were not wanting. Through the ages some Jews would periodically follow the global confrontation of great powers with breathless attention, convinced that the "wars of Gog and Magog" had already begun. The wars between Persia and Byzantium in the sixth and seventh centuries, the Arab conquest that humbled them both, the Mongol invasions of the thirteenth century, the explosive expansion of the Ottoman Turks in the fifteenth—all these could suddenly trigger such thinking.[15] We may note, parenthetically, that as late as the nineteenth century the Napoleonic wars were viewed as the wars of Gog and Magog in certain East European Hassidic circles. It is in Jewish apocalyptic literature, above all, that world events are often reflected most directly, and out of such texts we can sometimes even reconstruct minute and specific historical details. Yet there is no historiography here, only a desperate hunt for prophetic clues and signs of a final end to history in which, though the actors change, the scenario remains fundamentally the same.

Only in two instances in medieval Jewish historical writing can one detect a full awareness that something genuinely new has happened and that there is a special significance to the events themselves. In the four Hebrew chronicles of the Crusades written in the twelfth century there is not only a palpable sense of the terrifying shift in the relations between Jewry and Christendom that had ended in the destruction of entire Jewish communities, but an expression of astonished awe at this first instance of Jewish mass martyrdom on European soil.[16] In Abraham Ibn Daud's "Book of Tradition" (*Sefer Ha-Qabbalah*), the historical work of a Spanish philosopher which, despite its title, is far more than the usual compendium of the chain of rabbinic authority, there is a keen awareness of the movement of Jewish spiritual and cultural centers, first from Babylonia to Egypt, North Africa, and the Iberian Peninsula, and, in his own time, from Muslim to Christian Spain.[17]

But Ibn Daud and the Crusade chroniclers are, in this respect,

exceptional rather than exemplary, and ultimately even they show
a marked tendency to pour new wine into old vessels. Confronted
with the intolerable—the gruesome scenes of Jewish mass suicide
in the Rhineland, in which, by mutual consent, compassionate
fathers took the slaughterer's knife to their children and wives and
then to themselves rather than accept baptism—the chronicles of
the Crusades turn repeatedly to the image of Abraham ready to
slaughter Isaac at Mount Moriah. The *Akedah*, the "binding of
Isaac," becomes both paradigm and leitmotiv throughout this
literature, and performs a vital function for the generation of the
survivors. To be sure, the chroniclers are well aware of the objective difference. Writing of what happened in the city of Mainz, one
of the chroniclers, Shelomoh bar Shimshon, cries out:

Who has heard or seen such a thing? Ask and see: Has there ever
been an *akedah* like this in all the generations since Adam? Did eleven
hundred *akedot* take place on a single day, all of them comparable to
the binding of Isaac son of Abraham? Yet for the one bound on
Mount Moriah the world shook, as it is stated: "Behold the angels
cried out and the skies darkened." What did they do now, why did
the skies not darken and the stars not dim . . . when on one day . . .
there were killed eleven hundred pure souls, including babes and
infants . . . ? Wilt Thou remain silent for these, O Lord! [18]

But at the very same time that Moriah served as a foil for Mainz,
with the difference set into the sharpest relief, on a deeper level
the appeal to the Binding of Isaac also provided the desperately
needed understanding of what had occurred. The catastrophe
simply could not be explained by the stock notion of punishment
for sin, for the Ashkenazic communities of the Rhineland were
holy communities, as their own response to the crisis had demonstrated. Precisely here, however, lay the bridge to Abraham. The
factor that emerged as common to the martyrs and to the father
of the Jewish people was that the faith of both was put to the
supreme test, and this was not because the generation of the Crusades was unworthy but, on the contrary, because of its very

perfection. Thus, while the horror remained vivid it was no longer absurd, and grief, though profound, could be at least partly assuaged.

As for Ibn Daud's *Sefer Ha-Qabbalah*, in a subtle study accompanying his critical edition of the text, Gerson Cohen has argued plausibly that its esoteric purpose was to offer a messianic interpretation of history in whose climax Spain was to play a central role. At the same time, he has also demonstrated the remarkable degree to which, continuing a mode already manifest in classical rabbinic literature, Ibn Daud understood history by viewing it schematically. Ibn Daud was obsessed with "symmetry in history," especially when it came to historical chronology. Such alleged symmetries in the past served him as keys to future patterns as well, and he would discover or impose them even if it meant tampering with biblical and Talmudic data. To choose but one type of chronological equation out of many more intricate ones—this one based upon the number seven and its multiples—according to Ibn Daud, both the First and Second Temples stood for exactly 427 years; the First Temple was built in seven years and destroyed after a seven-year siege, while the Second Temple fell after seven years of Jewish subjection to Rome and revolt against it; the period of destruction of the First Temple began twenty-one years before its actual end, and this was later balanced by a twenty-one year period for the building of the Second Temple. Confronted with this kind of historical algebra (and it is by no means restricted to Ibn Daud), Professor Cohen's succinct remark is fully applicable to other aspects of Jewish historical thinking in the Middle Ages. "Schematology," he writes, "always betrays a very superficial interest in the events themselves, but a deep desire to unravel their meaning and their place in the plan of history as a whole."[19]

If, until now, I have dwelt exclusively on actual historical works, that is because their existence cannot be ignored. Within a broader perspective, however, these must be seen as fulfilling a subsidiary, even peripheral role. Historiography never served as a primary vehicle for Jewish memory in the Middle Ages. Most ordinary

chronicles and historical texts were neglected and forgotten, unless
(and here I refer again to the literature of the "chain of tradition")
they were of halakhic significance, or were embedded in juridical
or theological works. Most medieval Jewish historical writings,
such as they were, went down to oblivion, and most of those in our
hands today had to be rediscovered and published by scholars in
modern times. Should you really want to know what was the
medieval historical legacy available to Jewish readers after the
year 1500, you need only glance at the development of Hebrew
printing, then already in full sway. In addition to the ever-popular
Yosippon, only four historical works written before 1500 were
printed during the entire course of the sixteenth century: *Seder
'Olam Rabba* and *Seder 'Olam Zuta*, *Iggeret R. Sherira*, and Ibn
Daud's *Sefer Ha-Qabbalah*.[20] This was the entire library of post-
biblical historical writing that remained in general circulation
from all the preceding generations. In the Middle Ages, as before,
Jewish memory had other channels—largely ritual and liturgical
—through which to flow, and only that which was transfigured
ritually and liturgically was endowed with a real chance for survival and permanence.

The basic rituals of remembrance were still those which, biblical
in origin, had been significantly expanded in rabbinic halakhah.
These provided a shared network of practices around which clus-
tered the common memories of the people as a whole. And so the
great historical festivals of Passover, the Feast of Weeks and
Tabernacles remained central, but these did not exhaust the historical conjunctions of the Jewish calendar. There was Purim, with
its festive reading of the Book of Esther, and Hanukkah, sometimes accompanied by the reading of the so-called *Megillat Antiochus* (the "Scroll of Antiochus").[21] Three annual fast-days with
special liturgical features were linked to the destruction of the
Temple—the 10th of Tebet, when Jerusalem came under Babylonian siege, the 17th of Tammuz, when its walls were breached,
and the climactic 9th of Ab (*Tish'ah be-'Ab*) when, according

to tradition, both the First and Second Temples were destroyed, yet another example of the need for historical symmetry.[22]

Still, we should not be too hasty in attempting to generalize about the medieval Jewish awareness of time and history merely from the universal observance of such historically oriented holy days. It is important to recognize that virtually any given "historical" component in medieval Judaism could also contain, or be accompanied by, opposing elements.

Along with the annual calendar we find no less than three major systems of chronology in simultaneous use among medieval Jews: the Era of Creation, the era of the destruction of the Second Temple, and the Seleucid Era (the so-called *minyan shetarot*, or "era of contracts," also known as *minyan yevani*, or "Greek era").[23] By its very nature each era not only conjured up a very different quantitative span of time; it had qualitatively different historical resonances. Of the three, only the fall of the Temple brought one back to a vital point in Jewish history. The *anno mundi*, still in use today, refers to a cosmic event. The Seleucid Era had absolutely nothing Jewish about it. It commenced with a profane event in Hellenistic history (the conquest of Babylonia by Seleucus Nicator in 312 B.C.E.) that could not possibly have had any meaning for medieval Jews and had probably been long forgotten.[24] While it is easy to understand that the Seleucid reckoning was originally adopted by Jews, along with other peoples, as a convention and convenience, it is significant that no formal move was made to abolish it until the sixteenth century.[25]

Just as medieval Jews had more than one chronological principle for dating events, so they related to historical time in more than one dimension. Neither the usual "linear" nor "cyclical" category alone will suffice to describe their experience, which partook of each in special ways. Having already underscored the importance of the public reading of Scripture in impressing the biblical past upon the consciousness of Jews, we must also realize that the very incorporation of those ritualized public readings had also endowed that same past with the inevitably cyclical quality of liturgical time. True, Joseph had lived many ages ago, but in the fixed rhythm of the synagogal recital he is in prison this week, next week he will be released, next year in the very same season both events will be narrated once more, and so again in every year to come. A similar merging of historical and liturgical time, of verticality and circularity, was obviously present also in the historical festivals and fasts to which we have alluded. To be sure, all this is still far removed from any notion of an "eternal return" or of mythic time. The historical events of the biblical period remain unique and irreversible. Psychologically, however, those events are *experienced* cyclically, repetitively, and to that extent at least, atemporally. Nor were all Jewish holidays historically based to begin with. Rosh Ha-shanah and Yom Kippur are, at their core, numinous annual rites of repentance and atonement in which, on the deepest personal and collective levels, the sinful "history" of the old year is abolished to make way for a fresh and new beginning. Biblically, the Sabbath may have one rationale in Creation and another in the Exodus. Along the way it came to be experienced as a day beyond the bounds of historical time, and eventually even as a weekly anticipation of the end of time, of messianic stasis.

These reflections are only meant to indicate that not everything in Jewish tradition bore the stamp of history, and that a mere listing of commemorative observances cannot yield us what we want to know. To fully probe the memory-banks available to medieval Jews nothing less would suffice than a thorough re-examination of the entire range of Jewish liturgy and ritual, so heavily charged with intricate associations to past and future, and indeed of the entire gamut of Rabbinic law and custom as well. Such a task cannot be undertaken here. In any case, the real questions lie, not so much in what was available to stimulate and mold collective memory, as in the dynamics of the process itself. Yet it is this very aspect that proves the most elusive. Holy days, rituals, liturgies— all are like musical notations which, in themselves, cannot convey the nuances and textures of live performance.[26] Aware of the extreme difficulty in trying to penetrate those inner experiences, we can still try to identify several features that relate to our major theme.

We may safely assume, for example, that what was "remembered" had little or nothing to do with historical knowledge in any sense that we would assign to such a phrase. The Jews who mourned in the synagogue over the loss of the Temple all knew a date of the month, but I doubt if most knew or cared about the exact year when either the First or Second Temples were destroyed, let alone the tactics and weapons employed. They knew that Babylonians and then Romans had been the destroyers, but neither Babylon nor Rome could have been historical realities for them. The memories articulated in dirges of great poetic power were elemental and moving, but phrased in modes that simply bypass our notions of "knowing history." Here is a short selection from a long lament for the 9th of Ab which reveals just one way in which Jewish collective memory could structure itself:

A fire kindles within me as I recall—*when I left Egypt*,
But I raise laments as I remember—*when I left Jerusalem*.

Moses sang a song that would never be forgotten—*when I left Egypt*,
Jeremiah mourned and cried out in grief—*when I left Jerusalem*.

The sea-waves pounded but stood up like a wall—*when I left Egypt*,
The waters overflowed and ran over my head—*when I left Jerusalem*.

Moses led me and Aaron guided me—*when I left Egypt*,
Nebuchadnezzar and the Emperor Hadrian—*when I left Jerusalem*...[27]

It is the antiphony of the hammering refrain that first catches our attention. The "memory" of being exiled from Jerusalem is established and heightened by a repeatedly inverted comparison with the exodus from Egypt, the archetypal locus of Jewish historical reference. The appearance of Hadrian rather than Titus or Vespasian is interesting, but apart from that the lament is almost devoid of concrete historical details. That which is remembered here transcends the recollection of any particular episode in an ancient catastrophe. It is rather the realization of a structural contrast in Jewish historical experience, built around the dramatic polarity of two great historical "departures" (Egypt/Jerusalem—Exodus/Exile), each with its obvious though unstated clusters of meanings and implications. Most striking of all is the continual speech in the first person singular ("I left Egypt"; "I left Jerusalem") in lieu of an ancestral "they" or even a collective "we." We should be quite mistaken, I think, were we to attribute this usage merely to the liberties of poetic diction. The deliberate use of "I" is more serious than that, and it points to a larger phenomenon.

For whatever memories were unleashed by the commemorative rituals and liturgies were surely not a matter of intellection, but of evocation and identification. There are sufficient clues to indicate that what was suddenly drawn up from the past was not a series of facts to be contemplated at a distance, but a series of situations into which one could somehow be existentially drawn. This can perhaps be perceived most clearly in that quintessential exercise in Jewish group memory which is the Passover Seder. Here, in the course of a meal around the family table, ritual, liturgy, and even culinary elements are orchestrated to transmit a vital past from one generation to the next. The entire Seder is a symbolic enactment of an historical scenario whose three great acts structure the Haggadah that is read aloud: slavery—deliverance—ultimate redemption. Significantly, one of the first ritual acts to be performed is the lifting up of a piece of unleavened bread (*matzah*) before those assembled, with the declaration: *Ha laḥma 'anya*—"*This is the bread of affliction* which our forefathers ate in the Land of Egypt." Both the language and the gesture are geared to spur, not so much a leap of memory as a fusion of past and present. Memory here is no longer recollection, which still preserves a sense of distance, but reactualization.[28] It is this quality that impels the "I" in the *Tish'ah be-'Ab* lament as well, and nowhere is the notion brought forth more vigorously than in a Talmudic dictum central to the Passover Haggadah itself. "In each and every generation let each person regard himself as though *he* had emerged from Egypt."[29]

Potent as such mechanisms may have been, they still revolved around ancient memories, for the only universally accepted holy days, rituals, and liturgies, were those which referred to events up to the destruction of the Second Temple. Another large stratum of the past was added by the Talmud and the Midrashic literature. For most Jews, to whom absorption in Talmudic study was at the very heart of Jewish *paideia*, not only the juridical teachings of the rabbis, but their real or legendary biographies, rendered them familiar figures in a landscape of memory where the boundaries between history and legend were never sharply drawn. But the Talmud itself had reached its final form around the year 500 of the Common Era. It remains for us to inquire into the efforts made by Jews in the Middle Ages to preserve the remembrance of events that had been experienced, not by generations long past, but by themselves.

In this context I should like to identify four characteristic vehicles of medieval Jewish memory, each of which can tell us something about the mentality that created them.

The single most important religious and literary response to historical catastrophe in the Middle Ages was not a chronicle of the event but the composition of *seliḥot*, penitential prayers, and their insertion into the liturgy of the synagogue. Through such prayers the poet gave vent to the deepest emotions of the community, expressed its contrition in face of the divine wrath or its questions concerning divine justice, prayed for an end to suffering or vengeance against the oppressor, and, in effect, "commemorated" the event. A very large number of medieval historical *seliḥot* have survived.[30] While some contain actual names and descriptions of events, most do not. The poetic forms themselves militated against too literal a concern with specific details, while in general the poet could take it for granted that the community knew the "facts." For later generations, however, it was different. Even modern scholars, with all the tools of research available to them, will sometimes have difficulty in determining to which particular event a certain *selihah* refers.

Memorbücher — "Memorial Books" — flourished especially, though not exclusively, among Ashkenazic Jews. Kept for centuries in the archives of the community, into such volumes were inscribed not only the names of famous rabbis and communal leaders, but records of persecutions and lists of martyrs to be read aloud periodically in the synagogue during memorial services for the dead. Most *Memorbücher* were confined to the past of the local community. Others were wider in scope. The famous *Memorbuch* of Nuremberg, begun in 1296 and running up to 1392, contains, in addition to a poem on the building and dedication of the synagogue and lists of communal benefactors with prayers in Hebrew and in Old French, a martyrology that summarizes persecutions in Germany and France from the First Crusade of 1096 to the Black Death of 1349.[31] Yet although *Memorbücher* may contain important historical information, they cannot be regarded as historiography. Typically, their major purpose was to preserve the names of those for whose souls communal prayers were to be offered in the house of worship.

"Second Purims" were instituted in Jewish communities the world over to commemorate a deliverance from some danger or persecution.[32] I will cite only a few random examples, merely to indicate their diffusion and the variety of circumstances that could give birth to them. Thus, in Muslim Spain in the year 1038 a battle was fought near the village of El Fuente by the armies of Granada and Almeria. The vizier of the Kingdom of Granada was a Jew, the great Hebrew poet, scholar, and statesman, Samuel Ibn Nagrela, the only instance in the Middle Ages where a Jew occupied such a position of power. He had ample reason to fear that should Granada be defeated it would mean not only his personal downfall, but that of the entire Jewish community. Accordingly, when the Granadan forces were victorious he declared a Second Purim, and sent forth copies of a magnificent Hebrew poem he had composed for the occasion to Tunis, Palestine, and Babylonia, asking that the Purim be celebrated there as well.[33] The Purim of Narbonne in Southern France originated in the deliverance of the community in 1236 when an anti-Jewish riot, sparked after a Christian fisherman was killed by a Jew in a private quarrel, was subdued by the governor of the city.[34] In "Saragossa" (actually Syracuse in Sicily), either in 1380 or 1420, a Jewish apostate named Marcus revealed that the Jews had removed the Torah scrolls from their cases before the latter, according to custom, were shown to the king during a royal procession. Regarding this as an insult, the king decided to have the cases inspected on the next occasion. Meanwhile, we are told, Elijah the prophet warned of the danger and the scrolls were put back. When the king returned, the scrolls were found to be present, the community was saved, and Marcus was hanged, thus giving rise to the "Purim of Saragossa," which was still celebrated centuries later in various communities of the Ottoman Empire.[35] In 1578 Dom Sebastian, the young king of Portugal, landed with a crusading army in Morocco. The Jews were forewarned by two Marranos that if he proved victorious he intended to baptize them all by force, just as had been done to the whole of Portuguese Jewry in 1497. When Sebastian was defeated and killed at the Battle of Alcazarquebir, the Jews of Morocco instituted a Second Purim called, variously, "Purim Sebastiano" or "Purim de los Cristianos."[36]

A great many other such "Purims" are known, and almost all of them share certain common features. Unlike the original, biblical Purim, these never became national holidays. They were always local in character or, at most, they were observed over a certain geographic area. For all of them the original Purim served as a paradigm, and the new events were interpreted accordingly. Apart from certain additional prayers the most distinctive aspect of these Purims was the composition of a *megillah*, a "scroll" narrating the events, consciously modelled in style, structure, and even language upon the Scroll of Esther in the Bible. Here is one instance. In 1524 the governor of Egypt Ahmed Shaitan revolted against the Turkish sultan Suleiman the Magnificent, imprisoned twelve prominent Jews in an effort to extort money, and threatened to annihilate all the Jews of Cairo. His revolt, however, was crushed by the sultan's forces and he was beheaded. These events gave rise to the "Egyptian Purim," celebrated each year on the 28th of Adar with the public reading of the so-called *Megillat Mizrayim*, the "Scroll of Egypt."[37] Anyone familiar with the opening verses of the biblical book of Esther will not fail to recognize its deliberate paraphrase in the following:

Now it came to pass in the days of Suleiman the king, this is King Suleiman who reigned in Turkey, and the Levant, and Greece, and in many other provinces, that in those days, when King Suleiman sat upon the throne of his kingdom which was in Constantinople, the great city. . . .

Just as they created Second Purims, so medieval Jewish communities instituted special fast-days which, like the *selihot* that accompanied them, recalled those more bitter occasions when there was no deliverance.[38] I should like now to focus closely upon the rather extraordinary career of just one such special fast.

In May of the year 1171, in the French town of Blois, a Christian servant alleged that he had seen a Jew throw the corpse of a child into the river Loire. No corpse was ever found, but the forty Jews residing in Blois were imprisoned. The affair was further complicated by the fact that the ruler Count Thibaut, was having an affair with a Jewess, Polcelina, which aroused the jealousy of the count's wife, while other Christians resented the lady's influence at court. All now conspired to bring about the destruction of the community. Attempts at bribery were ineffectual. The servant was put through a dubious ordeal by water, after which his testimony was declared to be true. Offered the choice of baptism, most of the Jews, including Polcelina, chose to die. On the 20th of Sivan, May 26, 1171, thirty-two Jews, seventeen of them women, were burned at the stake.[39]

These, then, are the bare outlines of the first ritual murder accusation in continental Europe. The martyrdom at Blois made an enormous impression on contemporaries. In addition to two Hebrew prose accounts a number of *seliḥot* were composed. Upon hearing the tragic news the greatest Jewish authority of the age, Rabbi Jacob Tam (known as Rabbenu Tam), declared the day of the burning a perpetual fast. At the end of a prose narrative of the event written by Ephraim of Bonn we read:

Wednesday the 20th of Sivan 4931 [i.e., 1171 C.E.] was accepted by all the communities in France, England and the Rhineland as a day of mourning and fasting, of their own will, and at the behest of the illustrious scholar our master Jacob son of Rabbi Meir [Tam] who wrote letters to them and informed them that this day is worthy to be declared a fast-day for all our people, and this fast shall be greater than the Fast of Gedaliah ben Ahikam, for it is a day of atonement. These are the words that our master wrote, and thus is it proper, and thus did the Jews accept it.[40]

To appreciate the subsequent fate of this fast-day of the 20th of Sivan, we must now leap forward almost five centuries in time, from France to Eastern Europe.

In 1648, in Poland and the Ukraine, there erupted the great wave of Cossack pogroms led by Bogdan Chmielnitzky in which hundreds of Jewish communities were devastated, and thousands were killed, sold into captivity, or left destitute. For the Jews of Eastern Europe 1648 marked a blow whose scars were never healed.

As after the Crusades, so now, several chronicles were composed, as well as a considerable number of *seliḥot* and other liturgical poems. It has been pointed out that although the situation of Polish Jewry during the pogroms was quite different from that of the Jews of the Rhineland during the First Crusade, the two were homologized, and the writers depicted the slaughter of 1648 as a *repetition* of the martyrdom of the Crusades.[41]

This typological equation is significant in itself, but there is more to be said. In the *Megillat 'Efah* (the "Scroll of Terror"), an account of the Cossack massacres by Rabbi Shabbetai Katz, we read:

Therefore I have ordained for myself and for the coming genera-tions of my descendants a day of fasting, sorrow, mourning and lamen-tations *on the twentieth day of the month of Sivan* ... because this day has been the beginning of persecution and pain ... and because (on this day) afflictions were doubled ... *for the persecution of 4931 [1171] was on the same day* ... and I have composed these *selihot* and laments with tears and supplications, so they may be recited on this day in each and every year ....[42]

What was apparently initiated by Shabbetai Katz as a private fast-day was quickly accepted as a general one. When the Council of Four Lands, the governing body over the whole of Polish Jewry, met in Lublin in 1650, "they took it upon themselves and their posterity to fast throughout the Four Lands *on the twentieth day of the month Sivan,* each and every year. ..."[43]

The *selihot* composed by Shabbetai Katz were recited in Lithu-ania. In Poland proper the communities began to follow the custom of another prominent rabbinic leader of the time, Yom Tob Lipmann Heller. Unlike Shabbetai Katz, Heller took old *selihot,* among them two that had been composed in the twelfth century after the burning in Blois, and ordained that these be recited on the 20th of Sivan for the pogroms of 1648. The reason he gave is of surpassing interest:

What has occurred now is similar to the persecutions of old, and all that happened to the forefathers has happened to their descendants. Upon the former already the earlier generations composed *selihot* and narrated the events. *It is all one.* Therefore I said to myself—I shall go and glean among them, "for the fingernail of the former generations is worth more than the belly of the later ones" [*Yoma* 9b]. Also be-cause by reciting their prayers it will help our own to be accepted, since one cannot compare the words uttered by the small to those of the great. And thus their lips will move in the grave, and their words shall be like a ladder upon which our prayer will mount to heaven.[44]

Although, at the insistence of various persons, Yom Tob Lipmann Heller also wrote some new prayers of his own, his first view prevailed throughout Poland and spread beyond. Eventually, in most standard prayerbooks almost none of the *seliḥot* specially composed for the Cossack massacres remained.[45] For the 20th of Sivan which, to the eve of World War II, was still observed in Eastern Europe as a commemoration of 1648, only the medieval *seliḥot* were recited, and thus the cycle was closed.

I have dwelt in some detail on the peregrinations of the fast-day of the 20th of Sivan because, as a case study, it affords several insights into the workings of Jewish collective memory in the Middle Ages. In retrospect we are struck by the following elements:

1. The longevity of the original fast of Blois, which had obviously been carried to Eastern Europe through the waves of Ashkenazic migration into the Polish expanse and which, though instituted in the twelfth century, was still observed in the seventeenth.

2. The primacy of liturgy and ritual over historical narrative. There is no real evidence that, over the centuries, the prose accounts of the Blois tragedy were known to any but isolated individuals.[46] The fast, by contrast, was observed by entire communities.

3. The power of a commemorative observance such as the fast of the 20th of Sivan to preserve the essential memory of an event, without necessarily preserving its historical details.

4. Resistance to novelty in history. The pronounced tendency, after 1648, to fit the recent catastrophe into the mold of past tragedies, so dramatically expressed in Yom Tob Lipmann Heller's conviction that the *seliḥot* composed almost five centuries earlier were quite sufficient to embrace the contemporary event as well, "for it is all one."

5. The almost fortuitous character of the commemoration of

what happened at Blois. One can readily imagine what would have occurred had Rabbenu Tam not seen fit to call for a perpetual annual fast. The event might well have left no trace on posterity. The fact is that other major and cataclysmic events, including large-scale massacres or expulsions of entire Jewries, did not find their place in the calendar, and so did not survive in memory.

The features I have just enumerated are by no means exceptional. They are characteristic of medieval Jewish thinking, and correlate easily with similar traits that have emerged previously in our discussion on other grounds. In sum, memories of post-Talmudic events were partial and uneven at best, and there was no concerted effort to remember more.

There were three highways of religious and intellectual creativity among medieval Jews—halakhah (jurisprudence), philosophy, and Kabbalah—each of which offered an all-embracing orientation, and none of which required a knowledge of history in order to be cultivated or confirmed. These alone led to ultimate truths and to spiritual felicity. By comparison the study of history seemed at best a diversion, at worst—a "waste of time."

None of the other factors usually put forth to explain the relative indifference of medieval Jews to historical knowledge will suffice. It has been stated repeatedly that suffering and persecutions numbed their historical consciousness, or that they wrote little or no history because, lacking a state and political power, ordinarily the prime subjects of history, they had nothing to write about. It has even been suggested that there was little historiography because Jews had neither royal chroniclers nor monks who would devote themselves to such tasks. Such explanations, however, prove to be self-liquidating. All these factors remained equally true of the Jewish people in the sixteenth century. Yet in that time there was a sudden and unique flowering of Jewish historical writing that surpassed, in scope and in quality, almost anything that had appeared among the Jews since Graeco–Roman times.

3

IN THE WAKE OF
THE SPANISH EXPULSION

Among the riches and pleasures of joyous Asia I find myself a poor and wearied traveler, amidst the abundance of gold and fatness of the burning land of Africa, a wretched, famished and thirsty exile. Now Europe, O Europe, my hell on earth, what shall I say of you . . . ?

—Samuel Usque, *Consolation for the Tribulations of Israel*

As for the histories of Spain—the poor were always guests at our house and the exiles gathered under the shelter of our roof. The dear and distinguished Spanish Jews continually passed among us . . . and they related to me the entire great and terrible Spanish expulsion. . . .

—Elijah Capsali of Crete, *Seder 'Eliyahu Zuta*

Furthermore, tell me the reason for the fall of the Jews since ancient times . . . for behold, I have found their fall to be neither in a natural way, nor due to divine punishment. For we have seen and heard of many nations that have transgressed and sinned more than they and were not punished, but on the contrary—they succeeded with the greatest success. . . .

—Solomon Ibn Verga, *Shebet Yehudah*

But precisely because nothing in this book of mine has consequences for the laws of purity and impurity, or what is prohibited or permitted, I was impelled to write it, and the Lord God knows that it is not my intent to glorify myself or boast about it, for even little schoolchildren could compose a book like this. And I have not written it for the great scholars who are filled with Torah like pomegranates, but only for ordinary householders, immature students like myself. . . .

— David Gans, *Zemaḥ David*

And to distract yourself in an hour of depression, you have available to you *Yosippon, Zemaḥ David*, Ibn Daud's *Sefer Ha-Qabbalah, Sefer Yuḥasin, Shebet Yehudah*, and the histories of Joseph Ha-Kohen and Elijah Capsali. . . .

— Joseph Delmedigo [recommending books for reading to the Karaite Zerah b. Menahem]

The resurgence of Jewish historical writing in the sixteenth century was without parallel earlier in the Middle Ages.

Within the span of a hundred years no less than ten major historical works were produced by Jews: Solomon Ibn Verga's *Shebet Yehudah* ("The Scepter of Judah"), a precociously sociological analysis of Jewish historical suffering generally, and of the Spanish Expulsion in particular, expressed through a series of imaginary dialogues set within the framework of a history of persecutions;[1] Abraham Zacuto's *Sefer Yuḥasin* ("Book of Genealogies"), the most erudite and accurate history of rabbinic scholars that had yet appeared, interspersed with information on events in Jewish history, and with an appended chronology of world events;[2] Elijah Capsali's *Seder 'Eliyahu Zuta* ("The Minor Order of Elijah"), an elaborate history of the Ottoman Turks which incorporates both a history of Turkish and of Spanish Jewry, especially in the era of the Expulsion, as well as a separate work, *Sippurey Veneẓiah*, which is a chronicle of Venice and an account of the author's experiences in Padua from 1508 to 1515;[3] Samuel Usque's *Consolaçam as tribulaçoens de Israel* ("A Consolation for the Tribulations of Israel"), written in Portuguese, and encompassing the whole of Jewish history within the formal structure of a pastoral dialogue between three allegorical characters: "Ycabo" (Jacob— the Jewish people), "Zicareo" (Zachariah—the "Remembrancer"), and "Numeo" (Nahum—the "Consoler");[4] Joseph Ha-Kohen's *Dibrey ha-yamim le-malkhey Ẓarefat u-malkhey Bet Ottoman ha-Togar* ("History of the Kings of France and of the Ottoman Turkish Sultans"),[5] and his *'Emeq ha-Bakha* ("The Vale of Tears"), a history of Jewish sufferings since the fall of the Second Temple;[6] Gedaliah Ibn Yahia's *Shalshelet ha-Qabbalah* which, as its title indicates, is a "Chain of Tradition" that also contains information on historical events in Italy and elsewhere;[7] Azariah de' Rossi's *Me'or 'Einayim* ("Light for the Eyes"), not a narrative history, but a pioneering series of historial essays in which, among other matters, Hellenistic-Jewish literature (e.g., Philo of Alexandria and the "Letter of Aristeas") was first brought back to the attention of Jews, and both classical rabbinic aggadah and the Jewish calendar were first subjected to historical scrutiny and criticism;[8] and, finally, David Gans' *Zemah David* ("The Sprout of David"), divided into two parts, of which the first is a detailed chronology of Jewish history, and the second of world history.[9]

The contents of these works are, of course, far richer than a mere enumeration can suggest,[10] and each could easily merit a full and separate discussion. But it is not my present purpose to offer a comprehensive analysis of any one work of sixteenth-century Jewish historiography. These books are of interest not just for the historical data that can be extracted from any one of them, nor even for the light each may shed on the age in which it was written. Viewed in their ensemble, they can help us to further clarify certain overarching aspects of the relation of Jews to historical knowledge generally, both then and later.

Only in the sixteenth century do we encounter within Jewry a cultural phenomenon that can be recognized with little hesitation as genuinely historiographical. Though each of the ten works I have mentioned is quite distinct from the other, they also form a cultural and historical continuum. Of their eight authors, five were either exiles from Spain and Portugal or descendants of exiles (Ibn Verga, Zacuto, Usque, Joseph Ha-Kohen, Gedaliah Ibn Yahia). One, Elijah Capsali of Crete, was profoundly influenced by Spanish refugees who had come to the island. Only two, Azariah de' Rossi and David Gans, emerged out of a non-Sephardic milieu (Mantua and Prague, respectively). But Gans, writing toward the end of the sixteenth century, had already read and assimilated the works of his Sephardic predecessors. De' Rossi alone derived his decisive influences from other quarters.

The very provenance of most of these authors already hints at a larger pattern. In effect, the primary stimulus to the rise of Jewish historiography in the sixteenth century was the great catastrophe that had put an abrupt end to open Jewish life in the Iberian Peninsula at the end of the fifteenth, a link that is confirmed by explicit statements within some of the works themselves. Thus, for the first time since antiquity we encounter a ramified Jewish historiographical response to a major historical event. Nothing that had happened in the Middle Ages, not even the Crusader massacres, had engendered a comparable literature. In addition to the actual historical works, almost all branches of sixteenth-century Jewish literature contain direct or indirect references to the Spanish Expulsion of 1492, to the forced mass conversion of Portuguese Jewry only five years later, and to the sufferings of the refugees on land and sea.[11] Yet this was hardly the first expulsion of a European Jewry. The expulsion of the Jews of France in 1306, though not of the same dimensions, had been no paltry affair. Gersonides had characterized the number of French exiles as "twice those that emerged from Egypt."[12] Yet except for the passage in his commentary on the Pentateuch where this statement occurs, there are virtually no references in fourteenth-century Jewish texts to that great upheaval. The reverberations of the expulsion from Spain stand in glaring contrast.

Certainly there must have been more than one reason for this. But above all, we find a highly articulated consciousness among the generations following the expulsion from Spain that something unprecedented had taken place, not just that an abrupt end had come to a great and venerable Jewry, but something beyond that. Precisely because this expulsion was not the first but, in a vital sense, the last, it was felt to have altered the face of Jewry and of history itself. When Isaac Abravanel enumerated the sequence of European expulsions that began from England in 1290, he perceived the expulsion from Spain in 1492 as the climax and culmination of a process that had shifted the Jewish people, globally, from the West to the East.[13] That the largest and proudest Jewry in Europe had been uprooted was tragic enough. The larger significance of the Spanish Expulsion lay in the fact that, as a result, Western Europe had been emptied of Jews. When Abraham Zacuto compared the expulsions from Spain and Portugal with the earlier French expulsion, he understood the crucial difference. Relating that a forebear of his had been among the Jewish refugees from France in 1306 who had found an immediate haven across the border in Spain, he exclaims: "And from France they came to Spain. But we faced the enemies on one side, and the sea on the other!"[14]

That historical crisis should stimulate historical writing comes as no surprise. Indeed, we may find a pertinent example in the nexus between the rise of Italian humanist historiography and the breakdown of the republican system in the Italian city-states.[15] The resemblance ends there, however. Except for Azariah de' Rossi, we do not find that the spirit of Renaissance historical writing was really absorbed by sixteenth-century Jewish historiography, this even though some Jewish chroniclers drew considerable information from Italian histories. The elements of humanist culture that crop up in the works of Joseph Ha-Kohen or Gedaliah Ibn Yahia should not mislead us, for in the end they remain external trappings. Nor, as is commonly supposed, does the *Shebet Yehudah* of Ibn Verga betray influences of the Italian Renaissance.[16] Recent research has shown that Ibn Verga never came to Italy, but died in Flanders shortly after fleeing from Portugal in 1508.[17] If there are external influences in his book they should be sought, as I have long suspected, in the Iberian cultural milieu that was closest to him. In general, however, the dynamics of Jewish historiography after the Spanish expulsion are immanent to itself and related to what had happened within Jewry. Jews who, in the words of Tam Ibn Yahia, were "wallowing in the blood of the upheavals" wanted to understand the meaning of those upheavals and, as Ibn Verga put it—"Why this enormous wrath?" The answers were sought in a variety of ways. Significantly, a turning to the historical past was one of these.

Jewish historiography in the generations following the expulsion from Spain not only constitutes a novum; it was felt as such.

The awareness of novelty is expressed most vividly by Joseph Ha-Kohen, in an exultant passage that deliberately echoes the biblical Song of Deborah:

All my people is aware that no author has arisen in Israel comparable to Yosippon the priest, who wrote of the war of the land of Judea and of Jerusalem. The chroniclers ceased in Israel, they ceased, until I, Joseph, did arise, until I did arise, a chronicler in Israel! And I set my heart to write as a remembrance in a book the bulk of the troubles that have been visited upon us in gentile lands, from the day that Judah was exiled from its land until the present day.[18]

For all the hyperbole in this passage, it deserves special attention. Joseph Ha-Kohen was acquainted with the Jewish historical works of others and drew from them ("I gleaned among the sheaves after the harvesters, whatever my hand could find"). Nonetheless, he considers himself a new phenomenon. Since Yosippon (and let us remember that for him Yosippon was Josephus Flavius of the first century), "the chroniclers ceased in Israel." He states this as something of common knowledge ("all my people knows"), and in terms of the psychology revealed, his testimony is impressive. There is here a consciousness that to write history is something new for Jews, a new beginning after a very long interruption. Yet if, as he tacitly admitted, there were some historical works in former ages, whence did this feeling arise? What was there about his manner of writing history that enabled him to style himself the first Jewish historian since Josephus? Indeed, since we are concerned here not with Joseph Ha-Kohen alone, we may well broaden the question. What, in essence, were the novelties within sixteenth-century Jewish historiography as a whole?

To begin with, these works have a chronological and geographical scope far beyond anything that can be found previously. They do not focus merely upon this or that persecution or set of events, but attempt, within the limits of the data available to their authors, a coherent and consecutive survey of many centuries, in an expansive and detailed narration.

A new element is the prominence assigned to post-biblical Jewish history. For the first time we sense a keen interest in the entire course of Jewish history, from the destruction of the Second Temple down to the author's own time. The *Shebet Yehudah* is concerned almost exclusively with events that had occurred since the loss of Jewish independence and especially during the Middle Ages. Joseph Ha-Kohen begins his *'Emeq ha-Bakha*: "And it came to pass after all the glory had departed from Jerusalem." If he opens his *Dibrey ha-yamim* with "Adam begat Seth," it is only in order to establish the genealogies of the nations, and after half a page he plunges the reader into the seventh century of the Common Era and the rise of Islam. In Usque's Portuguese work there is a clear triple periodization, based, not upon the literary history of scholars and sages, but upon the larger rhythms of Jewish history: the periods of the First and the Second Temples, and a third period that comprises "all the tribulations Israel has suffered since the loss of the Second Temple, destroyed by the Romans, until this day." To this third period he devotes as much space as to the other two combined.

This points also to a new attitude toward the history of Jewry in exile. While, by and large, the Jewish historians of the sixteenth century believe, no less than did prior generations, that "for our sins were we exiled," and that "the fathers ate sour grapes and the teeth of the sons are set on edge," they do not regard this as a warrant to gloss over the history of those very sons. On the contrary, they lavish their attention upon it. Thus they bestow a new value upon the events that had transpired over the entire course of the Middle Ages. They seem to recognize instinctively that these events too have a meaning for the present and the future which cannot be grasped merely by focusing attention on ancient times, and that they are therefore worth recalling. All this marks a significant change in outlook.

A final novelty is the renewed interest in the history of the nations, especially of contemporary nations, in which a desire to know various aspects of non-Jewish history combines with an incipient recognition that Jewish destinies are affected by the interplay of relations between certain of the great powers. To these categories belong such works as Capsali's chronicle of Venice, and especially the large portions of his *Seder 'Eliyahu Zuta* which are devoted to the history of the Ottoman Empire.[19] In fact, for all its traditional theological presuppositions, the *Seder 'Eliyahu* may properly be regarded as a first, admittedly crude, attempt to write Jewish history within the framework of general history. From Joseph Ha-Kohen we possess not only the chronicle of the kings of France and Turkey, but his Hebrew translations (with insertions of his own) of Francisco López de Gómara's histories of the Spanish conquests of Peru and Mexico, the *Historia general de las Indias* (*Ha-Indiah ha-hadashah*) and *La conquista de México* (*Sefer Fernando Cortes*).[20] On another level mention should also be made of the various sections dealing with general history in Zacuto's *Sefer Yuhasin* and Ibn Yahia's *Shalshelet ha-Qabbalah*, and of course the entire second part of David Gans' *Zemah David.*[21]

Taken together, the features enumerated thus far are impressive enough, and for that very reason there is no need to inflate their proportions. Jewish historiography in the wake of the Spanish expulsion marks a leap forward when compared with what had preceded it. Within other perspectives its achievement tends to diminish. It never reached the level of critical insight to be found in the best of general historical scholarship contemporary with it. Moreover, although ten full-fledged historical works following so closely upon one another marked, for Jews, a period of relatively intense historiographical activity, they represented but a very small fraction of the sum of sixteenth-century Jewish literature.

Yet these reservations do not absolve us of our duty to evaluate this corpus of historiography within its own context, as one among a gamut of Jewish responses to the trauma of the expulsion from Spain. From this vantage point the work of the sixteenth-century Jewish historians may properly be seen as a significant attempt, however tentative, to pave the way among Jews toward a heightened concern with the historical dimension of their existence. In itself this phenomenon was laden with potential for future development and, had it continued, who knows where it might not have led. Seen in retrospect, however, we must conclude that it was an attempt that failed.

It was not, essentially, a failure of the historians, though their limitations are obvious in themselves and deserve to be spelled out.

With the exception of Azariah de' Rossi and Solomon Ibn Verga, they neither introduced new methods with which to examine the past, nor fundamentally new conceptual frameworks for an understanding of Jewish history. For all their innovations, they could not free themselves from conceptions and modes of thought that had been deeply rooted among Jews for ages. We have said that events since the destruction of the Second Temple received a new appreciation, and so they did. But in general these events were perceived as important, not because of any causal connection between them, but because the historians sought to find within them hints, configurations, and meanings that lay beyond them. For example, the historical episodes that Samuel Usque narrates derive their significance, not from any intrinsic links they might have to one another, but from his conviction that these events are fulfillments of biblical prophecies that predicted what would happen to the Jewish people in exile. By his own time, Usque believed, even the most dire of biblical prophecies had come to pass, and hence redemption was imminent. All that was lacking was that the Portuguese Marranos return openly to Judaism.

Messianic vibrations are discernible in both the *'Emeq ha-bakha* and *Dibrey ha-yamim* of Joseph Ha-Kohen, even though his messianism is generally restrained and often veiled. He himself hints at the messianic framework in a passage repeated in both books, declaring: "The expulsions from France as well as this exceedingly bitter exile [i.e., from Spain] have aroused me to compose this book, so that the Children of Israel may know what [the gentiles] have done to us in their lands, their courts and their castles, *for behold the days approach*." [22] Behind the "History of the Kings of France and of the Ottoman Turkish Sultans" there hovers a venerable apocalyptic tradition. Although, characteristically, Joseph Ha-Kohen does not allow apocalyptic elements to erupt into the foreground, his book is not a mere exercise in French and Turkish history, but an attempt to trace the age-old struggle between Christendom and Islam, whose leading contemporary standard bearers were perceived by him as France and the Ottoman Empire. The explicit history remains that of the French and the Turks; the tradition, however muted, that of Gog and Magog.[23]

The messianic theme of the *Seder 'Eliyahu Zuta* is so dominant as to leave no doubt of Elijah Capsali's intentions. The entire book is messianic history at its most exuberant. It is saturated with biblical messianic language and typologies, and the Turkish sultans are cast in the redemptive image of Cyrus the Great who had restored the Jews to the Land of Israel from their Babylonian captivity.[24]

In Ibn Verga's *Shebet Yehudah* there is, by contrast, not a trace of messianism, and in several respects its boldness and originality are impressive. Ibn Verga alone transfers the concept of "natural cause" (*ha-sibbah ha-tib'it*) from the sphere of philosophy and science to history, and it is he who went farthest in exploring the real mundane causes of the Spanish expulsion. Still, it remains a fundamental error to consider Ibn Verga, as have some, to be merely a rationalist with an essentially secular conception of Jewish history. The truth is that his use of "natural cause" by no means precludes or contradicts the notion of divine providence.[25] A close reading of the book will also reveal to what extent Ibn Verga was still bound by attitudes that had crystalized ages ago among the Hispano-Jewish aristocracy and no longer corresponded to the historical realities of his time.[26]

All these features, however regressive they might seem to modern eyes, do not detract from the achievements of the historians. A mixture of old and new is to be expected in the initial phases of almost any cultural development. The fate of sixteenth-century Jewish historiography was ultimately determined by an inheritance of a different order—the attitude among Jews toward historical works generally.

I have already stated in the last lecture that historiography never became a legitimate and recognized genre in medieval Judaism. This meant that except for Abraham Zacuto and Gedaliah Ibn Yahia, who continued to write within the familiar and accepted mold of the "chain of tradition," the Jewish historians of the sixteenth century found no available literary form into which to fit their work. Each, in fact, had to create his own individual forms. But though it made their task more difficult, it is not even this that ultimately defeated them. Something else had passed over from centuries gone by, namely, the relatively low esteem in which historical works of any kind had come to be held by most Jews. Despite their own occasional disclaimers (we shall examine these shortly), it can hardly be doubted that the sixteenth-century historians felt themselves engaged in something that was of high seriousness and purpose. Whether they were taken by the Jewish public as seriously as they deserved, or were even correctly understood, is questionable.

Though the reading public of the past is silent almost by definition, there are indirect ways of gauging the attitudes with which our authors had to contend. Most of the historical works under consideration are preceded by introductions overflowing with apology for the very fact that the writer is dealing with history at all, and offering a host of reasons to justify such a concern. Why was all this necessary? Because the historian knew very well the nature of the audience that awaited him. If even Zacuto, writing within a literary tradition in which distinguished rabbinic scholars of the past had already participated, still feels called upon to declare with a self-deprecatory shrug—"I cannot presume to say that it is a deep science, for because of my sins, as a result of the many persecutions and the want of a livelihood, I have neither strength nor wisdom"[27]—then how much more is there need for special pleading when David Gans presents his detailed chronology of the gentile nations.[28] These and other apologies go far beyond conventional literary protestations of modesty. Here it is not really the author's capacities that are at issue, but *the value of the enterprise itself*. All the introductions sound a common note. It is as though the historian were saying in the same breath: "Dear reader, although both of us know that what I am writing is unimportant, nevertheless it is important ...."

A somewhat whimsical but revealing example of another kind can be found in the first edition of *Dibrey ha-yamim* (Sabbionetta, 1554). We recall the exultant cry of Joseph Ha-Kohen in his preface to the work, "The chroniclers ceased, they ceased ... until I arose." But in old printed books it is worthwhile to read all the preliminary matter. In this instance, along with the author's introduction, the following verses are inscribed:

When the author's nephew, Zerahiah Halevi,
saw the glory of this book, and the nectar of its honeycombed words,
the Lord lifted his spirit and he began to speak.
So he opened his mouth with song and hymn, and declared:
Let anyone who delights in a time that was before ours
take this chronicle and read it when his sleep wanders....[29]

Faint praise this, one might say, in a poem purporting to extol the book! Certainly we understand that there is a biblicism lurking behind Zerahiah Halevi's lines (Esther 6:1—"On that night the king's sleep wandered, and he commanded to bring the book of records and chronicles ..."). But it is also more than a neat turn of a biblical phrase, and deserves to be taken seriously. Historical chronicles are to be read "when sleep wanders" (*bi-nedod shenah*), for otherwise such reading is a frivolous waste of time that could otherwise be devoted to the serious study of sacred texts. In fact, Zerahiah's attitude was by no means unusual. Despite Tam Ibn Yahia's veneration for *Yosippon*, he was at pains to add in his introduction to the work that especially "the merchants who are immersed in temporal successes, and who have not turned to the Torah in their leisure time, will delight in reading it."[30]

Of all the historical works, Ibn Verga's *Shebet Yehudah* was to

enjoy the widest popularity. I have examined no less than seventeen different editions printed from the mid-sixteenth century to
the early nineteenth, and there may be others. What was at the
heart of this extraordinary success? How was the book read, and
what did its readers see in it? Did they perceive its radical character? I think one may safely assume that only isolated readers
grasped Ibn Verga's intentions in exploring the Spanish expulsion
and the situation of Jews in Christian society. There are sufficient
indications that what seems central to us in the book was not what
attracted most readers, but rather other matters.[31] It is interesting,
for example, to follow the metamorphoses in the texts of the title
pages of the *Shebet Yehudah*, for these were aimed at focusing the
reader's attention on what were considered the highlights within.
Already in the title page of the first edition (Adrianople, 1553),
published more than four decades after Solomon Ibn Verga's
death, the following description of the book is given (the words
are not of the author, but of the editor, Joseph Ibn Verga, or the
printer):

> This is a book of the generations of Israel, and of the many misfor-
> tunes that have come upon the Jews in the lands of the nations. . . .
> And so it tells of the blood libel, how many times its falsehood was
> revealed and made public, and Israel emerged delivered. Similarly, it
> speaks of religious disputations that were held in the presence of
> kings, as well as the ceremony of installing the princes [i.e., the
> exilarchs] in various periods. . . . Finally, it depicts the structure of
> the Temple and its inner precincts, the service of the High Priest
> when he came to his chamber before the Day of Atonement, and the
> order of the Passover sacrifice, which we shall yet see with our own
> eyes, as we were promised by our Creator, the Lord of compassion.

What is so frustrating about this harbinger of the modern pub-
lisher's blurb is the fact that technically each detail is correct, yet
the total impression is so far removed from what we perceive to be
the inner spirit of the book. By the time we come to the third
edition, a Yiddish translation printed in Cracow in 1591 "for

ordinary householders, men and women" (*far gemayne baale-batim, man un vayber*), we can see from the title page that the *Shebet Yehudah* has been transmuted perceptually into a standard piece of edifying folk literature:

One will find in it marvelous stories of what happened to our fathers in exile, and how many times they underwent martyrdom, the book also specifying in which times and in which countries it all happened, so that a person's heart will be roused to the fear of God. May the Blessed Lord in His infinite mercy and grace continue to keep His people from all evil calamities, and send us the redeemer, Messiah son of David, speedily and in our own days.

More examples could be brought, but the point remains. The attitude toward historiography among sixteenth-century readers was no different, by and large, from what it had been in prior ages. An historical work was regarded as something pleasant and divert-ing in moments of leisure, and at best a source of moral uplift. Works concerned with the history of gentile nations were still described generically as "books of wars" (*sifrey milḥamot*), and in halakhic literature opinions continued divided as to whether one is permitted to read them, and when, and in what language.[32]

Still, one Jewish historical work of the sixteenth century, though not a chronicle, was received with sufficient seriousness to produce some very interesting repercussions. I have in mind Azariah de' Rossi's collection of historical and antiquarian essays, entitled *Me'or 'Einayim*. Unlike the other books with which we have been dealing the *Me'or 'Einayim* has no links to the Spanish expulsion and the spiritual crisis it provoked. It is rather the fruit of a cre-ative encounter, in the mind of an Italian scholar-physician, be-tween Jewish tradition and Italian Renaissance culture. Unlike so many other books written by Italian Jews that display a veneer of humanistic learning, here the humanist spirit has penetrated the very vitals of the work, and only here do we find the real begin-nings of historical criticism. The *Me'or 'Einayim* remains the most audacious Jewish historical work of the sixteenth century. Its

essential daring lies in Azariah's reluctance to set up predeter-
mined boundaries between his general and his Jewish knowledge,
in his readiness to allow a genuine confrontation between the two
spheres, and in his acceptance of whatever conclusions seemed to
flow out of it.

For our present discussion the most instructive aspect of the
book lies in what it reveals about the audience and the spiritual
climate of the time. Throughout his writing Azariah shows himself
particularly sensitive to public opinion. He writes with utmost
care, and is even prepared to make certain compromises so long
as they do not involve basic principles. Time and again he pauses
in order to comment on the objections he anticipates from his
potential readers. Thus, in speaking of various Talmudic references to the massacre of Alexandrian Jewry:

Let us now turn back to the city of Alexandria. Our eyes behold
three different passages concerning it, for the Jerusalem Talmud has
stated that the evil murderer was the emperor Trajan . . . and the
Babylonian Talmud in tractate *Sukkah* said it was Alexander of
Macedon, while in tractate *Gittin* it changed its opinion to write that
it was Hadrian. And if we have now begun to investigate the [his-
torical] truth of these matters, that is not because of the thing in itself,
for what was—was [*mai de-havah havah*], but only because we are
concerned that the words of our sages in relating well-known events
should not appear to contradict one another.[33]

Later on, in the same chapter:

At any rate, even were we to admit that some stories reached the
ears of the sages with some distortion, and that this is how they related
them to us, that in no way diminishes their stature. . . . And even
though this chapter consists mostly of inconsequential investigations
[*haqirot shel mah be-khakh*], for it will be said "what was—was, and
there is in it no relevance to law or observance," still, the refined soul
yearns to know the truth of everything.[34]

And again, in his strictures on the computation of the traditional Jewish era of Creation:

Before we leave this subject it will become clear that the manner in which they, of blessed memory, computed the years, was considered a noble science whose worth was known and proclaimed by every enlightened person. However, I can foresee that you will say to yourself, dear reader: "But surely such an investigation is completely farfetched [*hilkheta de-meshiḥa*; literally, "law for the time of the Messiah"] and even worse, for what have we to do with all this, considering that what was—was, several thousand years ago or more?"[35]

There are many more such passages in the *Me'or 'Einayim*, and they demonstrate vividly the reactions that Azariah expected from his readers. He was wary of them on two counts. His overall concern was that they had a low opinion of any historical investigation. "What was—was." This phrase seems to sum up for him the prevalent Jewish mood, and it surfaces so frequently in the book as to be a recurring refrain. More specifically, however, he suspected that some of the contents of the book would be construed as a denigration of the Talmudic sages.

As it turned out, his worries were not in vain. The book was attacked even as it was being printed.[36] In various Italian Jewish communities it was placed under rabbinic ban.[37] Admittedly, the Italian ban was a mild one, and concerned only the book and not its author. Elsewhere reactions were harsher. Rumblings were heard from Prague and from as far away as Safed in Palestine.[38] Some rose in defense of the book. But the question remains—what, in essence, stirred up the tempest? Azariah was no heretic, but a respected scholar whose personal piety was not in question. Mantua was a center of Jewish intellectuals well attuned to the cultural currents of the time. Indeed, most of the Italian rabbis who signed the ban were not obscurantists, but men of fairly broad secular culture.

Could it really have been Azariah's debunking of the rabbinic legend about the gnat that entered Titus' head through the nose and finally killed him?[39] Azariah himself relates that there were Jews who sharply criticized this passage in his book and regarded what he had done as an insult to the sages. But could the critique of such a legend really have seemed like a novelty in the sixteenth century? Did there not already exist long and recognized traditions within Judaism, whether philosophical or kabbalistic, which could not accept rabbinic legends literally, but strove to reinterpret them rationally or mystically, at times to the most radical extremes? In what manner, then, had Azariah de' Rossi overstepped the bounds?

I would suggest that the answer lies, not in the fact of Azariah's criticism, but in its source, method, and conclusions. Philosophic and kabbalistic critiques and interpretations of aggadah possessed an age-old legitimacy, although, to be sure, there still remained Jews in Azariah's time who would not accept even these.[40] The essential innovation in Azariah's approach lay in his attempt to evaluate rabbinic legends, not within the framework of philosophy or Kabbalah, each a source of truth for its partisans, but by the use of profane history, which few, if any, would accept as a truth by which the words of the sages might be judged. Worse than that, Azariah ventured to employ non-Jewish historical sources for this purpose, drawn from Greek, Roman, and Christian writers. Above all, he did not flinch from the conclusions that emerged out of the comparison, even when these affected so sensitive an area as calendar computation. As for Titus' gnat, Azariah would not reinterpret the legend metaphorically or allegorically, nor did he spiritualize it in any way in order to salvage it. Citing Roman and other historians as to the actual date and cause of Titus' death, he dismissed the story as historically *untrue*. Such historical critiques could not yet be tolerated, let alone assimilated, by Azariah's Jewish contemporaries. On the contrary, it is perhaps a token of the flexibility of Italian Jewry that the ban upon the book (it was not pronounced against Azariah himself, and only required that special permission be obtained by those who wanted to read it) was not enforced stringently, and there were some who continued to read it in subsequent generations. Azariah's experiment, however, remained his alone. There were no heirs to his method.

In a sense this lack of impact characterized sixteenth-century Jewish historiography as a whole. Reviewing all the elements we have discussed, our conclusion is not without its ironies. Were I to sum it all up, I would state bluntly that far from providing evidence for the spread among Jews of an active interest in the writing and reading of historical works, let alone of the growth of a new historical consciousness, a close study of sixteenth-century Jewish historiography only sets into sharper relief the degree to which traditional attitudes toward history continued among the majority. In retrospect we see the phenomenon as a sudden flowering and an equally abrupt withering away. It stimulated no further bursts of historical interest and creativity and had no real parallel for the next two hundred years. The chronicles that were written subsequently broke no new ground.[41] The vehicles of memory were still those we discussed in the preceding lectures. At the end of the sixteenth century those Jews who still sought the meaning of Jewish historical suffering and of the length of exile found it in the Kabbalah of Isaac Luria and his disciples, which spread out from a Galilean hill town to rapidly conquer the Jewish world. It is surely more than coincidence that a people that did not yet dream of defining itself in mundane historical categories should now have found the key to its history in an awesome metahistorical myth of a pronounced gnostic character. That myth declared that all evil, including the historical evil that is Jewish exile, had its roots before history began, before the Garden of Eden was planted, before our world existed, in a primal tragic flaw that occurred at the very creation of the cosmos itself. [42]

I do not mean by this to imply in any way that sixteenth-century historiography and Lurianic Kabbalah stood in a consciously competitive relationship in which the latter was "victorious." Though both were ultimately related to the Spanish expulsion, each represented a separate response with its own inner dynamics. If I juxtapose the two, it is not in order to suggest an organic lateral relationship, but because of what the juxtaposition reveals about the mentality of Jews. That the historiographical effort proved abortive, while the Lurianic myth permeated ever-widening circles in Jewry, seems to me a fact of no small consequence for an understanding of important facets of that mentality. Whatever Lurianic Kabbalah may have meant to Jews (and Gershom Scholem has unveiled for us both its conceptual grandeur and overwhelming pathos), its rapid reception by the Jewish world is significant in itself. Clearly, the bulk of Jewry was unprepared to tolerate history in immanent terms. It is as though, with the culminating tragedy of the expulsion from Spain, Jewish history had become opaque, and could not yield a satisfactory meaning even when, as among most of the historians, it was viewed religiously. Patently, however, Jews were spiritually and psychologically prepared for that which Lurianic Kabbalah offered them—a mythic interpretation of history that lay beyond history, and that seemed to endow the individual with the power to participate actively in hastening its messianic liquidation.

For us, both the Jewish historiography and the Kabbalah of the sixteenth century have become "history." Not only are we equidistant from both; we study both—historically. But if some of us style ourselves historians and do not aspire to be kabbalists, that should not indulge us in the illusion that we have salvaged the one over the other. Modern Jewish historical scholarship has other roots.

The fact that, in 1794, the *Me'or 'Einayim* was reprinted in Berlin by the *Maskilim*, the proponents of Jewish enlightenment, should not mislead us in this respect. By that time the general revolution that is modern critical historiography was about to burst forth in Germany. The *Historisches Journal* had already appeared in Göttingen for more than two decades, Barthold Niebuhr was eighteen years old, and Leopold Von Ranke would be born a year later. The modern Jewish historian is not the heir of Azariah de' Rossi, but of these men and others. The mode whereby he came into this inheritance has implications of its own, as do the uses he has made of it. We are now perhaps in a position to consider these matters.

4

MODERN DILEMMAS

Historiography and Its Discontents

You really had brought some traces of Judaism with you from the ghetto-like village community. It was not much and it dwindled a little more in the city and during your military service; but still, the impressions and memories of your youth did just about suffice for some sort of Jewish life. . . . Even in this there was still Judaism enough, but it was too little to be handed on to the child; it all dribbled away while you were passing it on.

—Franz Kafka, *Letter to His Father*

Thus a situation has developed which is quite paradoxical in human terms: The barriers of the past have been pushed back as never before; our knowledge of the history of man and the universe has been enlarged on a scale and to a degree not dreamed of by previous generations. At the same time, the sense of identity and continuity with the past, whether our own or history's, has gradually and steadily declined. Previous generations *knew* much less about the past than we do, but perhaps *felt* a much greater sense of identity and continuity with it. . . .

—Hans Meyerhoff, *Time in Literature*

As a professional Jewish historian I am a new creature in Jewish history. My lineage does not extend beyond the second decade of the nineteenth century, which makes me, if not illegitimate, at least a *parvenu* within the long history of the Jews. It is not merely that I teach Jewish history at a university, though that is new enough. Such a position only goes back to 1930 when my own teacher, Salo Wittmayer Baron, received the Miller professorship at Columbia, the first chair in Jewish history at a secular university in the Western world. More than that, it is the very nature of what and how I study, how I teach and what I write, that represents a radically new venture. I live within the ironic awareness that the very mode in which I delve into the Jewish past represents a decisive break with that past.

It is significant that the first real attempt in modern times at a coherent and comprehensive post-biblical history of the Jews was made, not by a Jew, but by a French Huguenot minister and diplomat, Jacques Basnage, who had found refuge in Holland.[1] His *Histoire du peuple Juif depuis Jésus Christ jusqu'à présent, pour servir de continuation à l'histoire de Joseph* appeared in seven volumes in Rotterdam, 1706–11, and in an expanded fifteen-volume edition in the Hague, 1716–21. Very few people will read Basnage's history today, and for good reason. It is far from our notion of critical history. There is no archival research. The basic Christian presumption of an ultimate conversion of the Jews remains. Yet nothing like it had been produced before, and Basnage knew this. "I dare to say," he writes, "that no historian has appeared among the Jews themselves who has gathered together so many facts concerning their nation."[2] He complains of the paucity of reliable materials. Of those Jewish works that were devoted to the "chain of tradition" he observes that, "attached only to the succession of the persons through whom the tradition has passed from mouth to mouth, they have preserved the names and have often neglected the rest."[3] In his opinion even the Jewish historians of the sixteenth century "seem to have little knowledge of former centuries."[4] It is a measure of the state of affairs in the eighteenth century that when a Dutch Jew, Menahem Man Amilander, wrote his *Sheyris Yisroel*, a history of the Jews in Yiddish published in 1743, he had to rely heavily on Basnage, whom he may have read in a Dutch translation.[5]

With the spread of Haskalah, the movement for secular enlightenment among the vanguard of German Jewry in the second half of the eighteenth century, we find a vague consensus among its leading proponents that a knowledge of history is somehow desirable for Jews. In Naftali Zvi Weisel's call for a new Jewish curriculum entitled *Dibrey Shalom ve-'Emet* ("Words of Peace and Truth") which appeared in 1782, the study of general history is included, but in these characteristic terms:

It is fitting that those who go to the house of study also learn the order of the generations and the events that have occurred . . . for this knowledge helps one to understand the words of the Torah which has related to us how the first descendants of Noah conquered the earth, and the names of countries based on the names of their first inhabitants, and the affairs of Nimrod and Assyria . . . but in the eyes of anyone not versed in the ancient chronicles all these things are like a dream with no interpretation.

[A knowledge of history] also helps one toward the love and fear of the Lord, for when one knows the customs of these early nations . . . he will understand why the Lord did not choose them and why, among all of them, he chose Abraham alone. . . .

Similarly, a man becomes wiser out of a knowledge of history, for when he reads the deeds of the men of all the nations that existed before us he will see the effects of good counsel through which entire nations prospered . . . and by contrast he will see the effects of bad counsel through which great kingdoms declined and collapsed. All such knowledge will ennoble the heart of man and lift him above the thoughts of the mass of day-dreaming fools.[6]

But, as you may have already suspected from this passage, it was not the Haskalah that fathered modern Jewish historiography,

though it unwittingly helped prepare the ground for it by hastening the secularization of significant segments of the Jewish people,
first in Germany and then elsewhere. The Haskalah itself did not
attain a conception of history fundamentally different from those
that prevailed earlier. When the *Me'assef*, the Hebrew journal of
the German Haskalah, began publication in the fall of 1783, the
editors decided to include biographies of famous Jews in each issue.
Yet in the first volume they expressed their concern lest the reader
"will say to himself—'this is of no purpose'—and we will be
suspect in his eyes as though it were our intention to fill the journal
with trivial matters."[7] Accordingly, they printed an article entitled
"A Word to the Reader on the Utility of the History of Life in
Former Times and the Knowledge Allied to It"[8] in which, though
a case is made for historical study, it is clear that history has as
yet no intrinsic value, but is still completely subordinate to traditional concerns. Four kinds of utility are specified: "philosophical"
(one develops a more rational comprehension of one's own tradition by learning about others); "literary" (for a proper understanding of Torah and Talmud); "political" (it will be useful for
business); and "moral" (by sustaining a true judgment of what is
right and wrong through a knowledge of the mores of other peoples). In spirit, if not in detail, we are thrown back to the apologia
of the sixteenth-century Jewish historians.

From Weisel and the *Me'assef* to the famous manifesto published by Immanuel Wolf in 1822 and entitled *On the Concept
of a Science of Judaism* is a span of forty years, a biblical generation. Yet it represents a drastic leap into a new kind of thinking.

The immediate background is well known. Already in 1817 the
twenty-three year old Leopold Zunz had written an article, "Etwas
über die rabbinische Literatur," in which a program was sketched
for an historical study of the whole of Jewish civilization, expressed through all the varieties of its literature, which would take
its place as an integral component of human knowledge as a
whole.[9] In 1819 Zunz and a group of other young German Jews
that included the as-yet unbaptized Heinrich Heine established a

"Verein für Cultur und Wissenschaft der Juden" (Society for Culture and the Scientific Study of the Jews). Wolf's essay appeared in 1822 in the journal of the society, the *Zeitschrift für die Wissenschaft des Judenthums.*[10]

Here, suddenly, there are no apologies. History is no longer a handmaiden of dubious repute to be tolerated occasionally and with embarrassment. She confidently pushes her way to the very center and brazenly demands her due. For the first time it is not history that must prove its utility to Judaism, but Judaism that must prove its validity to history, by revealing and justifying itself historically. When, throughout the essay, Wolf repeatedly invokes the term *Wissenschaft*—"Science"—he has in mind specifically the new critical historical spirit and historical methodology that were sweeping Germany and that would soon become one of the hallmarks of nineteenth-century European thought. With this in mind, we read:

Scientific knowledge of Judaism must decide on the merits and demerits of the Jews, their fitness or unfitness to be given the same status and respect as other citizens. This alone will make known the inner character of Judaism and separate the essential from the accidental, the original from the late addition.

And, in the most unequivocal terms:

It is manifest everywhere that the fundamental principle of Judaism is again in a state of inner ferment, striving to assume a shape in harmony with the spirit of the time. But in accordance with the age, this development can only take place through the medium of science. *For the scientific attitude* [read: the *historical* attitude] *is the characteristic of our time.*

Wolf's explicit agenda for a Wissenschaft des Judentums posited a three-fold hierarchical endeavor: "First, the textual study of Judaism; second, a history of Judaism; third, a philosophy of

Judaism," with the latter obviously to emerge out of the second. Whence did this new spirit among Jews arise?

It should be manifest by now that it did not derive from prior Jewish historical writing or historical thought. Nor was it the fruit of a gradual and organic evolution, as was the case with general modern historiography whose roots extend back to the Renaissance. Modern Jewish historiography began precipitously out of that assimilation from without and collapse from within which characterized the sudden emergence of Jews out of the ghetto. It originated, not as scholarly curiosity, but as ideology, one of a gamut of responses to the crisis of Jewish emancipation and the struggle to attain it.[11]

I do not use the term "assimilation" in a negative sense. I have already stressed that the creative assimilation of initially foreign influences has often fructified the Jewish people. The culture of Spanish Jewry is only the best known, but far from the only example of this. What is new in the absorption by Jews of the historicist perspectives of nineteenth century European culture is not the fact of the encounter, but its content and consequences.

In this sense a comparison with the Middle Ages can be instructive. Though there were many levels of interaction between medieval Jews and their cultural environments, the most daring and profound intellectual synthesis took place in the realm of philosophy. As against this we remarked, in the second lecture, that the absence of interaction in the sphere of historiography remains all the more telling. In modern times we have, as it were, the reverse. There has been little genuine interpenetration between Jewish and general philosophy, but a deep and ubiquitous interaction with modern historicism. By this I mean simply that while there was a common realm of discourse and mutual influence among Jewish, Muslim, and Christian philosophy in the Middle Ages, this has not been true of Jewish and general philosophy in modern times. The primary intellectual encounter between Judaism and modern culture has lain precisely in a mutual preoccupation with the historicity of things. As a result there is not a field of Jewish learning today which, to the degree that it is modern, is not "historical," and only insofar as they are historically oriented have the disciplines of Jewish scholarship impinged upon cognate fields of general scholarship, a process now constantly accelerating.

There is also an intrinsic difference, however, in the nature of the medieval and modern confrontations. In the Middle Ages Jewish philosophers felt a need to effect a reconciliation between a Greek truth and a revealed Judaism of whose truth they were equally convinced. Those Jews in the early nineteenth century who first felt an imperative to examine Judaism historically did so because they were no longer sure of what Judaism was, or whether, whatever it was, it could still be viable for them. Edouard Gans, one of the animating spirits of the Verein, wrote in a presidential report:

> The break with the intimacy of the old existence has indeed oc-curred, but the deeper return to this intimacy has not taken place. The enthusiasm for religion and the genuineness of the old relationships has vanished, but no new enthusiasm has broken forth, no new set of relationships has been built.[12]

The modern effort to reconstruct the Jewish past begins at a time that witnesses a sharp break in the continuity of Jewish living and hence also an ever-growing decay of Jewish group memory. In this sense, if for no other, history becomes what it had never been before—the faith of fallen Jews. For the first time history, not a sacred text, becomes the arbiter of Judaism. Virtually all nineteenth-century Jewish ideologies, from Reform to Zionism, would feel a need to appeal to history for validation. Predictably, "history" yielded the most varied conclusions to the appellants.

To be sure, the achievements of Wissenschaft were not merely coextensive with its origins nor, by now, is the corpus of modern Jewish historiography limited to a Wissenschaft which it has tran-scended and even rejected in significant ways.[13] The full story of modern Jewish scholarship has yet to be told in detail, even in its

externals. Merely to contemplate the mundane obstacles that lay
in its path during the nineteenth century is to be dismayed in retrospect. Bibliographical and archival foundations had to be established where almost none existed. Post-biblical Jewish studies were
systematically excluded from the universities. Jewish scholars
knew from the start that they could not aspire to academic careers.
That they obstinately pursued their vocation in the face of adversi-
ties shared neither by their gentile counterparts nor by their more
favored successors today smacks of the heroic or the compulsive.
That despite the tendentious and apologetic motives behind so
much of nineteenth-century Wissenschaft the working scholar,
once absorbed in his research, produced so much of substance, is
remarkable. A climax to Wissenschaft and a measure of its success
may be seen in the very fact that Heinrich Graetz was able to offer
in his multivolume history, published between 1853 and 1870, a
synthesis that would have been inconceivable fifty years earlier.
In the twentieth century entirely new perspectives and avenues
were opened by such post-Wissenschaft historians as Simeon
Dubnow in Eastern Europe and Salo Baron in the United States,
and by those scholars working within the national revival of the
Jewish people in its own land, of whom Gershom Scholem, the
historian of Jewish mysticism, has had the most revolutionary
impact. By now the the available library of Jewish scholarship is
of formidable proportions, and ongoing research, international
in scope, expands continually.

In its totality modern Jewish historiography presents both a
general and a Jewish aspect, each of which can be a subject for
extended discussion. The first concerns its contribution as pure
scholarship to the sum of man's historical knowledge and understanding; the second, its place as a cultural and spiritual phenomenon within Jewry itself. I will focus only on the latter, and
even then, confine myself to a few selected problems.

One may well wonder at the outset whether Jewish historiography in modern times can be said to display any problematics of
its own. Historical objectivity, the nature of historical explanation,

the value of quantification—these and other questions cut across all historical disciplines. Precisely because modern Jewish historiography stands, by its own avowed principles, on common ground with all of modern historical research, it also shares every aspect of the current general malaise. Historians are criticized simultaneously by social scientists and philosophers. The very image of the historian in modern literature is, by and large, a tarnished one.[14] The historian of the Jews cannot be immune merely because of his subject matter.

Nonetheless, other problems have been neither shared nor common. Some arose out of purely historical circumstances, but even these indicate how the very same impulses can refract differently within a specific group. The fathers of Wissenschaft may have wholeheartedly accepted the philosophic and methodological assumptions of the new historical scholarship, yet in important ways they were out of phase with it. To take a simple example: Where German scholarship began with political and institutional history and only later turned to intellectual history, Wissenschaft focused first and foremost on the latter, for there seemed to be no Jewish political history to write about, and the social or economic history of the Jews was largely beyond its ken.[15]

More tragic and significant was the contrast between the respective context within which Jewish and gentile historians operated. The golden age of European historiography in the first half of the nineteenth century coincided with the dawn of modern nationalism and drew much of its élan from it. The German or French historian had a vital and honored place in the process of national awakening. At the very same time, however, Europe was demanding of the Jews alone that, as a condition for their emancipation, they cease to regard themselves as a nation and redefine themselves in purely religious terms. With few exceptions (Graetz was one of them) the scholars associated with Wissenschaft des Judentums willingly concurred. Accordingly, they reconstructed a Jewish past in which the national element was all but suppressed, and the hope for national restoration seemed an anachronism. Nor did the national language fare better. Wissenschaft performed prodigies of scholarship in the unearthing and analysis of Hebrew texts, and we owe much of the recovery of medieval Hebrew literature to its efforts. But where European scholars were garnering their medieval literatures with the assurance of possessing languages still spoken and secure for the future, the Jewish scholars neither foresaw nor particularly desired a revival of Hebrew. Introduced in his old age to a contemporary poet visiting from Russia, Zunz, who had devoted decades of his life to research in medieval Hebrew literature, is reputed to have asked him, "When did you live?"

If, fortunately, such problems have been left far behind, there are others of an almost intrinsic order that cannot so easily be relegated to a certain stage of development, for they are overarching.

There is an inherent tension in modern Jewish historiography even though most often it is not felt on the surface nor even acknowledged. To the degree that this historiography is indeed "modern" and demands to be taken seriously, it must at least functionally repudiate premises that were basic to all Jewish conceptions of history in the past. In effect, it must stand in sharp opposition to its own subject matter, not on this or that detail, but concerning the vital core: the belief that divine providence is not only an ultimate but an active causal factor in Jewish history, and the related belief in the uniqueness of Jewish history itself.

It is the conscious denial, or at least the pragmatic evasion, of these two cardinal assumptions that constitutes the essence of the secularization of Jewish history on which modern Jewish historiography is grounded. True, the revolution was already anticipated by Spinoza in the seventeenth century ("as for their continuance so long after dispersion and the loss of empire, there is nothing marvelous in it") [16] and in the eighteenth by Voltaire ("we shall speak of the Jews as we would of Scythians or Greeks") .[17] But the notion that Jewish history is on the same level of reality as any other history, subject to the same kind of causality and accessible to the same types of analysis, did not find its way into actual historical writing until the nineteenth century. Long after an essentially secular view of world history had permeated ever-widening European circles, a providential view of Jewish history was still held tenaciously, albeit for very different reasons, by Jews and Christians alike. Indeed, it has far from disappeared even now. The reason for the lag is apparent. Of all histories, that of the Jewish people has been the most refractory to secularization because this history alone, as a national history, was considered by all to be sacred to begin with. The point has been made forcefully by Karl Löwith:

There is only one particular history—that of the Jews—which as a political history can be interpreted strictly religiously. . . .
Christians are not an historical people. Their solidarity all over the world is merely one of faith. In the Christian view the history of salvation is no longer bound up with a particular nation, but is internationalized because it is individualized. . . . From this it follows that the historical destiny of Christian peoples is no possible subject for a specifically Christian interpretation of political history, while the destiny of the Jews *is* a possible subject of a specifically Jewish interpretation.[18]

Needless to say, that is not the course that modern Jewish historiography has taken. To underscore this, let me offer you a rather dramatic and, to my mind, fascinating contrast. In the dark year of 1942 a book was published in Fascist Rome by a German Jesuit scholar, Peter Browe, entitled *Die Judenmission im Mittelalter und die Päpste* ("The Mission to the Jews in the Middle Ages and the Popes"). True to its title, it was a thorough history of the Christian attempt to convert the Jews in the Middle Ages. The book was based on a wide variety of primary sources and was accompanied by dense and impeccable footnotes. It is still a standard work on the subject and remains of high interest. But most interesting of all is the last chapter, which deals with the manifest failure of the Christian mission to achieve its total goal. Some Jews had been converted everywhere, in Spain many; but medieval Jewry as a whole had not succumbed. This final chapter, which

Browe called "Die Gründe für den geringen Erfolg der Juden-mission" (The reasons for the meager success of the mission to the Jews) is divided into three parts. The first is "Die Gründe von Seiten der Christen" (The reasons from the Christian side—namely, what was there in the Christian approach that precluded a greater success). The second is "Die Gründe von Seiten der Juden" (The reasons from the Jewish side—to wit, what was there about the Jews that enabled them to resist). At this point Browe's hitherto consistent empiricism leaves him stranded. Having exhausted all the "reasons" he could find, Browe felt that the phenomenon was not yet fully comprehensible. The last part is entitled "Die Gründe von Seiten Gottes" (literally, "the reasons from God's side"). Perhaps, in the end, God himself did not want Judaism to be obliterated. In conclusion Browe wrote:

> This entire history of the Jewish people, its life and wandering throughout the centuries, the preservation of its race and peoplehood amid innumerable struggles and persecutions, cannot be explained out of purely political and sociological considerations. . . . Only out of faith can we in some way understand the solution. . . .[19]

I submit that no Jewish historian today, whatever his private feelings and beliefs, would bring himself to write an explicit "reasons-from-God" epilogue to a work of scholarship, and, lest you misunderstand, I am not necessarily advocating that it should be otherwise. I merely point out that what would be inconceivable in a history of the English, the French, or the Dutch is still possible in a serious twentieth-century historical work concerning the Jews.

If the secularization of Jewish history is a break with the past, the historicizing of Judaism itself has been an equally significant departure. It could hardly be otherwise. Western man's discovery of history is not a mere interest in the past, which always existed, but a new awareness, a perception of a fluid temporal dimension from which nothing is exempt. The major consequence for Jewish historiography is that it cannot view Judaism as something absolutely given and subject to *a priori* definition. Judaism is insepa-

rable from its evolution through time, from its concrete manifes-
tations at any point in history. Wissenschaft was still certain that
there must be an essential "Idea" of Judaism behind the shifting
forms that history casts up to our view, and believed that this idea
could be distilled by the historian. By now that nineteenth-century
philosophical idealism has been largely repudiated. Along the
way, the very notion of a "normative Judaism" has been seriously
and effectively challenged.[20]

Voices of protest have not been wanting. In the nineteenth century Samson Raphael Hirsch, the father of that so-called "Neo-
Orthodoxy" which was itself a response to emancipation, vehe-
mently opposed the relatively conservative Jewish Theological
Seminary in Breslau because of its commitment to historical scholarship, and personally attacked Graetz, who had once been his
disciple.[21] That late flower of Italian Jewish humanism, Samuel
David Luzzatto, a scholar with so great a passion for research that
he declared his readiness to hand old Hebrew manuscripts to Satan
himself if the latter would only edit and publish them, gazed with
dismay at the Jewish scholars in Germany and castigated them for
lacking "the faith which seeks to grasp the Torah and prophets
as the word of God, and to see in Jewish history the singular chronicle of a singular people."[22]

Perhaps the most sophisticated and best known disavowal of
historicism was made in the twentieth century by one of its most
original Jewish thinkers—Franz Rosenzweig. Rosenzweig's rejection of historical development as a primal category for an understanding of Judaism or the Jewish people is doubly impressive as
the conclusion of one who was neither unacquainted with what
modernity means, nor unaware of what the historical outlook
implies.[23] He had come back to Judaism from an assimilation that
had brought him to the brink of conversion to Christianity, and
had written his doctoral dissertation on "Hegel and the State" for
Friedrich Meinecke at the University of Berlin. Yet his *Star of
Redemption* posits that Jewry has already long achieved a condition of stasis through the observance of an atemporal law that has

removed it from the flux of history. Christendom is "eternally on the way"; the Jewish people alone experiences eternity in the midst of history itself.[24]

These examples among many already suggest that the historical outlook has by no means enjoyed an unqualified triumph within Jewry. What its place may be, and some of the factors that have determined it, may become clearer as we return to our point of origin in these lectures: the relation between Jewish historiography and Jewish memory.

Only in the modern era do we really find, for the first time, a Jewish historiography divorced from Jewish collective memory and, in crucial respects, thoroughly at odds with it.

To a large extent, of course, this reflects a universal and ever-growing modern dichotomy. The traditions and memories of many peoples are in disarray. At the same time, national history in the nineteenth-century sense has yielded increasingly to other thematic structures. If I continue to limit myself to the Jewish case that is not only because, as an historian of the Jews, I fancy that I know it best, but also because, as a Jewish historian, I find myself personally involved.

There are many within Jewry today who deplore the widespread decay of Jewish memory even while, perhaps symptomatically, sharing no real consensus as to its original or ideal content. Who, then, can be expected to step into the breach, if not the historian? Is it not both his chosen and appointed task to restore the past to us all? Though he did not have the Jewish historian in mind, Eugen Rosenstock-Huessy's description of the historical vocation might almost seem, fortuitously, to pose a particular challenge to him. "The historian," he wrote, "is the physician of memory. It is his honor to heal wounds, genuine wounds. As a physician must act, regardless of medical theories, because his patient is ill, so the historian must act under a moral pressure to restore a nation's memory, or that of mankind."[25]

Yet those who would demand of the historian that he be the restorer of Jewish memory attribute to him powers that he may not possess. Intrinsically, modern Jewish historiography cannot replace an eroded group memory which, as we have seen throughout, never depended on historians in the first place. The collective memories of the Jewish people were a function of the shared faith, cohesiveness, and will of the group itself, transmitting and re-creating its past through an entire complex of interlocking social and religious institutions that functioned organically to achieve this. The decline of Jewish collective memory in modern times is only a symptom of the unraveling of that common network of belief and praxis through whose mechanisms, some of which we have examined, the past was once made present. Therein lies the root of the malady. Ultimately Jewish memory cannot be "healed" unless the group itself finds healing, unless its wholeness is restored or rejuvenated. But for the wounds inflicted upon Jewish life by the disintegrative blows of the last two hundred years the historian seems at best a pathologist, hardly a physician.

That much is, or should be, obvious, and can be laid aside. It is when we approach the historian with more modest and sober expectations, within his proper sphere, so to speak, that a deeper rift is revealed.

Memory and modern historiography stand, by their very nature, in radically different relations to the past. The latter represents, not an attempt at a restoration of memory, but a truly new kind of recollection. In its quest for understanding it brings to the fore texts, events, processes, that never really became part of Jewish group memory even when it was at its most vigorous. With unprecedented energy it continually recreates an ever more detailed past whose shapes and textures memory does not recognize. But that is not all. The historian does not simply come in to replenish the gaps of memory. He constantly challenges even those memories that have survived intact. Moreover, in common with historians in all fields of inquiry, he seeks ultimately to recover a total past— in this case the entire Jewish past—even if he is directly concerned with only a segment of it. No subject is potentially unworthy of his interest, no document, no artifact, beneath his attention. We understand the rationales for this. The point is that all these features cut against the grain of collective memory which, as we have remarked, is drastically selective. Certain memories live on; the rest are winnowed out, repressed, or simply discarded by a process of natural selection which the historian, uninvited, disturbs and reverses.[26] The question remains whether, as a result, some genuine catharsis or reintegration is foreseeable.

Certainly at the present moment the very opposite seems to be the case. Gone is that optimistic assurance with which a Graetz or a Dubnow could feel that the whole of Jewish history can yield, if only in secular terms, a meaningful unified structure or a clear pattern of development. Even as we await the eighteenth (and by no means final) volume of Baron's monumental *Social and Religious History of the Jews*, we know that we are probably witnessing the last serious attempt by a single historian to embrace the whole of Jewish history. The sign of the times is the collaborative *World History of the Jewish People* now being published slowly and intermittently, each of whose volumes is a collection of independent historical essays that can claim, at best, a merely chronological unity. Whatever their obvious merits as summations of the current state of knowledge they cannot, even when completed, add up to an interpretation of Jewish history. No symphony was ever written by a committee.

Nothing has replaced the coherence and meaning with which a powerful messianic faith once imbued both Jewish past and future. Perhaps nothing else can. Indeed, there is a growing skepticism as to whether Jewish history can yield itself to any organizing principle that will command general assent. Delving into increasingly circumscribed yet complex areas of study the contemporary Jewish historian often accomplishes prodigies of scholarship even as, concomitantly, he is able to remove himself thereby from the "large" issues that only the whole can pose with any urgency—the uniqueness of Jewish historical experience (if not in a metaphysical then at least in an empirical sense); what was once called the "mystery" of Jewish survival through the ages; the relationship between

Jews and Judaism (is all of Jewish history "Jewish"?); the value of Jewish history itself, not for the scholar, but for the Jewish people. The Jewish past unfolds before the historian not as unity but, to an extent unanticipated by his nineteenth-century predecessors, as multiplicity and relativity. How could it be otherwise? More than a century-and-a-half ago Jewish scholars took the fateful step of re-examining the Jewish past from the angle of vision of Western historicism. By now, having faithfully pursued its course, modern Jewish historiography cannot but parallel its defeats as well as its triumphs.

Seen in this light the resistance or indifference of certain Jewish circles to modern Jewish historical scholarship becomes somewhat more comprehensible. The real issue, however, is broader and more serious. It is not that Jewish historiography has not affected the thinking of this or that group, but that although it constitutes the single most sustained Jewish intellectual effort in modern times, it has impinged so little upon modern Jewish thinking and perception generally. I do not think I exaggerate. Anyone familiar with what Jewish historical research has achieved must concede that this new knowledge and the perspectives it offers have hardly been faced, let alone internalized.[27] In effect, it is not modern Jewish historiography that has shaped modern Jewish conceptions of the past. Literature and ideology have been far more decisive. That this should be so seems to me sufficiently interesting to make one pause and reflect.

Surely the rejection of the historical vision cannot be shrugged off as due to mere ignorance or philistinism. Anti-historical currents within modern Jewry are themselves active forces, and are generated from different sources that have little else in common.

Those Jews who are still within the enchanted circle of tradition, or those who have returned to it, find the work of the historian irrelevant. They seek, not the historicity of the past, but its eternal contemporaneity. Addressed directly by the text, the question of how it evolved must seem to them subsidiary, if not meaningless.

An anti-historical attitude of a very different kind is expressed by those who have experienced modern Jewish existence as something so totally new that it demands the past be either forgotten or demolished. The deep ambivalence of modern Jews to the past is perhaps best discerned in modern Hebrew literature, which, even more than Yiddish or Anglo-Jewish letters, reflects the widest spectrum of modern Jewish sensibility. Here we find, on the one hand, the fiercest antagonism to the Jewish past, not as a personal idiosyncracy, but a major theme that runs from the Haskalah to the present. One of the purest instances will suffice. In the explosive short story by the Hebrew writer Haim Hazaz entitled *Ha-Derashah*[28]—"The Sermon"—a meeting of a kibbutz is held at which Yudka, who never speaks on such occasions, startles everyone by rising to unburden himself of thoughts he can no longer contain. Haltingly, at first, he declares what has been gnawing at him:

"I want to state," Yudka spoke with an effort in low, tense tones, "that I am opposed to Jewish history."

And then, when his stammering gives way to an articulate fury:

"I would simply forbid teaching our children Jewish history. Why the devil teach them about our ancestors' shame? I would just say to them: Boys, from the day we were exiled from our land we've been a people without a history. Class dismissed. Go out and play football."

And yet, concurrently, modern Hebrew writers have been gripped often by an aching nostalgia for a vanished Jewish past. Both impulses are present, repulsion and attraction, rejection and a sense of loss, iconoclasm and grief. It is not simple. Anti-historical attitudes alone cannot explain the lack of resonance that modern Jewish historiography has encountered. Many Jews today are in search of a past, but they patently do not want the past that is offered by the historian. The extraordinary current interest in Hassidism totally ignores both its theoretical bases and the often sordid history of the movement. The Holocaust has already engendered more historical research than any single event in Jewish history, but I have no doubt whatever that its image is being shaped, not at the historian's anvil, but in the novelist's crucible. Much has changed since the sixteenth century; one thing, curiously, remains. Now, as then, it would appear that even where Jews do not reject history out of hand, they are not prepared to confront it directly, but seem to await a new, metahistorical myth, for which the novel provides at least a temporary modern surrogate.

I have no obvious solution to offer for the various issues I have raised, nor do I regard them as external to myself. I am far from immune to the seductions of myth, and I fancy myself more aware than most of its place in the healthy life of a people. I freely admit that there are times when I myself question the value of studying the past, disturbing thoughts that come usually "when sleep wanders," and occasionally during the day. They have not altered my vocation, and I trust the admission will not dismay my students. I shall not conclude with a philosophical defense of history that will add little to the many already available. The following are only some very partial observations, bottles cast upon the waters for whatever destination they may find.

Modern Jewish historiography cannot address itself to those Jews who have never "fallen." The potential dialogue of the historian is with those who, consciously or unwittingly, have tasted of forbidden fruit and can never be the same. I think these are the majority. True, Franz Rosenzweig reclaimed his birthright without the aid of history, through a far more decisive experience in an orthodox synagogue in Berlin on the Day of Atonement. Franz Kafka, fallen modern Jew that he was, "with a fierce longing for forebears" that neither his own father nor the synagogue could assuage, read Graetz "eagerly and happily," yet another search that, like so much else in his life, never attained its goal.[29] Interestingly, it was Rosenzweig himself who declared: "There is no one today who is not alienated."[30]

Here it is different. When I spoke earlier of the coincidence of the rise of modern Jewish historiography and the decay of Jewish memory, I had in mind a specific kind of memory of the past, that of Jewish tradition. But hardly any Jew today is without some Jewish past. Total amnesia is still relatively rare. The choice for Jews as for non-Jews is not whether or not to have a past, but rather—what kind of past shall one have.

Yudka, who opposes Jewish history, has a past, only with an intermission of almost two millennia. It grinds to a halt with the fall of Masada in the second century and resumes again with the return to Zion in the late nineteenth. What happened in between is for him a nightmare best forgotten. The suburban Jewish past of the characters in the fiction of Philip Roth is also a Jewish past, only as meager as the span of a generation or two and infinitely more distasteful, because so much more trivial, than Yudka's. One could assemble an entire anthology of Jewish pasts in the modern world, some sublime, others pathetic and crippling. These are themselves realities. Consciously or not, they impinge on the lives of those who bear them, and ultimately on the Jewish people as a whole.

Whether in this welter of floating pasts the voice of the historian is heard depends on many factors, but the question itself is not without consequence. For all of one's justified mistrust of historical parallelism, it is hard to escape the feeling that the Jewish people after the Holocaust stands today at a juncture not without analogy to that of the generations following the cataclysm of the Spanish Expulsion. They, as we saw, ultimately chose myth over history, for reasons that it would be futile to question retroactively since its consequences cannot be undone. Today Jewry lives a bifurcated life. As a result of emancipation in the diaspora and national sovereignty in Israel Jews have fully re-entered the mainstream of history, and yet their perception of how they got there and where they are is most often more mythical than real. Myth and memory condition action. There are myths that are life-sustaining and deserve to be reinterpreted for our age. There are some that lead astray and must be redefined. Others are dangerous and must be exposed.

The burden of building a bridge to his people remains with the historian. I do not know for certain that this will be possible. I am convinced only that first the historian must truly desire it and then try to act accordingly. I shall not attempt a catalogue of remedies; I do not know them all myself. What historians choose to study and write about is obviously part of the problem. The notion that everything in the past is worth knowing "for its own sake" is a mythology of modern historians, as is the lingering suspicion that a conscious responsibility toward the living concerns of the group must result in history that is somehow less scholarly or "scientific." Both stances lead, not to science, but to antiquarianism. How historians write is also germane. What I have in mind need not involve us in the now tiresome debate as to whether history is an "art" or a "science," which merely perpetuates the fallacy that the content of an historical work can be separated from the form in which the historian presents it. The divorce of history from literature has been as calamitous for Jewish as for general historical writing, not only because it widens the breach between the historian and the layman, but because it affects the very image of the past that results. Those who are alienated from the past cannot be drawn to it by explanation alone; they require evocation as well.

Above all, the historian must fully confront a contemporary Jewish reality if he is to be heard at all. Yudka, for example, is very much part of that reality, and his demands are pressing. I understand Yudka very well, for in a sense he is transparent. His repugnance for Jewish history in exile derives, in part, from a conception of it as nothing but the history of how Jews died and the books they wrote. It is a view that was, in the main, fostered by Wissenschaft historians themselves. Jewish historiography has long outgrown it.[31] But the historian who thinks that all Yudka requires is a knowledge, easily assembled, that there was a rich and abundant Jewish life in the Middle Ages, or proof that Jews were far from passive in the face of history, is mistaken. For the same stuttering Yudka who is opposed to history also has keen, if unsophisticated, historical instincts. For example, he at least knows viscerally that Zionism was a revolt against Jewish messianism, and that the national awakening and the return to the land are, in the words that Hazaz gives him, "no continuity but a break, the opposite of what was before, a new beginning."

To address Yudka meaningfully, and all the many modern Jews who have experienced the other radical "breaks" that modern Jewish existence has entailed, some reorientation is required. The task can no longer be limited to finding continuities in Jewish history, not even "dialectical" ones. Perhaps the time has come to look more closely at ruptures, breaches, breaks, to identify them more precisely, to see how Jews endured them, to understand that not everything of value that existed before a break was either salvaged or metamorphosed, but was lost, and that often some of what fell by the wayside can become, through our retrieval, meaningful to us. To do so, however, the modern Jewish historian must first understand the degree to which he himself is a product of rupture. Once aware of this, he is not only bound to accept it; he is liberated to use it. This entire series of lectures has been, on one of its levels, a rejection of the pedigrees that some Jewish historians have tried to assign to themselves,[32] a recognition of the chasm that separates modern Jewish historiography from all the ways in which Jews once concerned themselves with their past.

Throughout these lectures, and especially in this final one, I have spoken unabashedly in inner Jewish terms. I trust, nevertheless, that in the end you will not regard the main issues raised as intramural. There are hardly any, I think, that cannot be translated and generalized, though that has not been my present aim. I will close in the same way, still with a few Jewish adjectives, though more lightly attached. You can easily remove them.

I have emphasized that modern Jewish historiography can never substitute for Jewish memory. But I am equally convinced that a historiography that does not aspire to be memorable is in peril of becoming a rampant growth. As the flood of monographs and books crosses my desk each year, I often wonder why a scholar chose this particular topic when, with the same linguistic and methodological equipment, he could have chosen another. Each time I hear that a young and promising scholar has "not published enough," something within me protests. The enterprise has become self-generating, the quest—Faustian.

Jorge Luis Borges tells a story, *Funes el memorioso* ("Funes the Memorious"), which haunts me largely because, though Borges did not intend it so (he called it a "metaphor of insomnia"), it looms as a possibly demonic parable for a potential dénouement to modern historiography as a whole.[33] It is a tale about an Uruguayan, Ireneo Funes, who, as the result of a fall from a horse at the age of nineteen, found that henceforth he could forget nothing, absolutely nothing. He tells Borges: "I have more memories in myself alone than all men have had since the world was a world." But I give you Borges' own words:

We, in a glance, perceive three wine glasses on the table; Funes saw all the shoots, clusters, and grapes of the vine. He remembered the shapes of the clouds in the south at dawn on the 30th of April of 1882, and he could compare them in his recollection with the marbled grain in the design of a leather-bound book he had seen only once, and with the lines of the spray which an oar raised in the Río Negro on the eve of the battle of the Quebracho. . . .

In effect, Funes remembered not only every leaf on every tree of every wood, but every one of the times he had perceived or imagined it. He determined to reduce all of his experiences to some seventy thousand recollections, which he would later define numerically. Two considerations dissuaded him: the thought that the task was interminable and the thought that it was useless. He knew that at the hour of his death he would scarcely have finished classifying even all the memories of his childhood. . . .[34]

The shadow of Funes the Memorious hovers over us all. Today, increasingly, historiography itself becomes the object of historical inquiry. Perversely, I have contributed to it here. Conceivably someday there could be a history of the history of historiography, and then a history of that, and so on in a continuing spiral. It is enough to tease us out of thought.

I pursue my work amid such ruminations. I do not know if the vast undertaking that is modern historical scholarship will prove an enduring one, either for Jews or for others. Solomon's ring, commissioned to make him happy when he was sad and sad when happy, was inscribed by the jeweller with the words, "This too shall pass." There may well come a time when a new consciousness will prevail that will wonder why so many of us were immersed in history, or it may not bother with us at all. Perhaps, in the end, it is such a thought that helps to keep me at my task. The very ability to conceive a time when men and women think differently than we, be it in the future or in the past, is the fruit of that historical consciousness which is ours in the present. We cannot avoid it without an inner violence and betrayal, even if we know that what we do may be only provisional. But that is all right. In the terrifying time in which we live and create, eternity is not our immediate concern.

Postscript: Reflections on Forgetting

(AN ADDRESS DELIVERED AT THE COLLOQUE DE ROYAUMONT, JUNE 3, 1987)

Prelude in a Tentative Mode

Months ago there had been some mention of a conference to be held while I will be in France, but since I have heard nothing further I forget about it entirely.

The actual invitation arrives in New York just as I am completing the semester at Columbia and preparing to teach for the first time at the École des Hautes Études. The theme: "Usages de l'oubli"—"The Uses of Forgetting." No, I have not misread it . . .

The topic tentatively assigned to me: "Hypertrophy of Memory; Forgetting of History." This I must reject. If at all, "Atrophy of Memory; Hypertrophy of History." But I shall rather have no title at all, or the vaguest one possible. Secretly, in fact, I would much prefer that the admirable Jacques Le Goff speak and I merely listen. But this is not to be. Having written about memory, I must now apparently atone for that act of presumption by speaking about forgetting. I accept this fate with trepidation. What can I say that is not already implicit in what I have written?

My initial panic is somewhat assuaged by a coincidence which, superstitiously, I choose to interpret as a favorable omen.

Only a few days before receiving notice of the conference I have bought and rapidly devoured two books by the great Russian psychologist Alexandr Romanovitch Luria. One is *The Man with a Shattered World: The History of a Brain Wound;* the other, *The Mind of a Mnemonist: A Little Book about a Vast Memory.* [1] Both, as you may know, are case histories, classics of psychiatric literature. Each is the mirror image of the other. Well, at least there will be something to think about on the plane to Paris . . .

I

The man whose world was shattered had been shot in the head during World War II at the Battle of Smolensk. Though he survived, he had lost most of his memory, his very capacity to remember. By sheer force of will and with incredible effort he began to write, a few sentences each day, over a period of some twenty-five years. Slowly, painfully, he was able to recover fragments of his past and even to arrange them in some meaningful order. But while this activity gave him a tenuous link to life, normal living was denied him. At one point he cries out: "I remember nothing, absolutely nothing! Just separate bits of information . . . but that's all! I have no real knowledge of any subject. My past has just been wiped out!"

The mnemonist, on the other hand, was endowed since childhood with a memory so prodigious that he astounded the psychologists who studied him and the audiences that came to see him perform on the stage.

The tragedy of the man wounded at Smolensk does not surprise us; we are accustomed to regard amnesia as pathological. Yet the phenomenon of the mnemonist was no less pathological. If the brain-damaged man could not remember, the mnemonist could not forget. And so it was even difficult for him to read, not because, like the man of Smolensk, he had forgotten the meaning of words, but because each time he tried to read, other words and images surged up from the past and strangled the words in the text he held in his hands. Referring to the mnemonist, whom he calls "S.," Luria states the problem succinctly:

Many of us are anxious to find ways to improve our memories; none of us have to deal with the problem of how to forget. In S.'s case, however, precisely the reverse was true. The big question for him, and the most troublesome, was how he could learn to forget.[2]

We are irresistably reminded of Nietzsche, who, already in 1874, proclaims the crisis of historicism in terms of illness: "We are all suffering from a malignant historical fever and should at least recognize the fact."[3] Again: "Life in any true sense is absolutely impossible without forgetfulness. . . ."[4] And, after these initial outbursts, this sober observation:

. . . we must know the right time to forget as well as the right time to remember, and instinctively see when it is necessary to feel historically and when unhistorically. This is the point that the reader is asked to consider: that the unhistorical and the historical are equally necessary to the health of an individual, a community, and a system of culture.[5]

Well, of course. The reader nods his head in agreement because the point is essentially banal. It also begs the question. Health, we might say, lies somewhere between the mnemonist and the man of Smolensk. But given the need both to remember and to forget, where are the lines to be drawn? Here Nietzsche is of little help to us. How much history do we require? What kind of history? What should we remember, what can we afford to forget, what must we forget? These questions are as unresolved today as they were then; they have only become more pressing. Nor, I am afraid, for reasons yet to be discussed, will we resolve them here or in the foreseeable future.

II

But we have already run far ahead of ourselves. Our basic terminology is as yet unripe. We cannot speak meaningfully of "forgetting" without simultaneously considering what we mean by "remembering." And so I shall make a provisional distinction between memory *(mneme)* and recollection *(anamnesis)*. Memory, for our purposes, will be that which is essentially unbroken, continuous. Anamnesis will serve to describe the recollection of that which has been forgotten. In true Jewish fashion I have, of course, borrowed these terms from the Greeks, specifically from Plato, where they refer not to history but to philosophic knowledge of the eternal Ideas. Except for those rare individuals whose souls have retained traces of their prenatal memories of the world of the Ideas, all true knowledge is anamnesis, all true learning an effort to recall what has been forgotten. There is a curious parallel to this in the Talmud [tractate *Niddah*], where we are told that the fetus in the womb knows the entire Torah and can see from one end of the world to the other. But at the very moment of birth an angel comes and slaps the infant on the mouth (in later legend he kisses him), whereupon he immediately forgets everything and (alas) must learn the Torah anew. Since there are scholars here who know the Greeks far better than I, I will commence, as is my custom, with the Jews, and work my way outward to more general considerations.

III

"The Uses of Forgetting." In the Hebrew Bible they are not to be found. The Bible only knows the terror of forgetting. Forgetting, the obverse of memory, is always negative, the cardinal sin from which all others will flow. The *locus classicus* is perhaps to be found in the eighth chapter of Deuteronomy:

> Beware lest you *forget* the Lord your God so that you do not keep His commandments and judgments and ordinances . . . lest you lift up your hearts and *forget* the Lord your God who brought you out of the land of Egypt, out of the house of bondage . . . And it shall come to pass if you indeed *forget* the Lord your God . . . I bear witness against you this day that you shall utterly perish. (Deut. 8:11, 14, 19)

This astonishing assumption, that an entire people cannot only be admonished to remember but held absolutely responsible for forgetting, is made as though it were self-evident. Yet surely, collective forgetting is at least as problematic a notion as collective memory. If we take it in a psychological sense it becomes virtually meaningless. Strictly speaking, peoples, groups, can only forget the present, not the past. That is to say, the individuals who comprise the group can forget events that occurred within their own lifetime; they are incapable of forgetting the past that preceded them, in the sense that the individual human being forgets earlier stages in his own life history. When we say that a people "remembers" we are really saying that a past has been actively transmitted to the present generation and that this past has been accepted as meaningful. Conversely, a people "forgets" when the generation that now possesses the past does not convey it to the next, or when the latter rejects what it receives and does not pass it onward, which is to say the same thing. The break in transmission can occur abruptly or by a process of erosion. But the principle remains. A people can never "forget" what it has never received in the first place.

Thus, if the man of Smolensk and the mnemonist have served us well as initial metaphors, they must not be allowed to linger as analogues. As the "life of a people" is a biological metaphor, so the "memory of a people" is a psychological metaphor—unless one personifies the group as an organism endowed with a collective psyche whose functions correspond in every way to that of the individual—which is to say, unless one chooses to read history with Freud and face the consequences of a now discredited psycho-Lamarckism.[6]

IV

What we call "forgetting" in a collective sense occurs when human groups fail—whether purposely or passively, out of rebellion, indifference, or indolence, or as the result of some disruptive historical catastrophe—to transmit what they know out of the past to their posterity. All the admonitions to "remember" and not to "forget," by which the Jewish people felt itself addressed, would have been of no avail if the rites and historical narratives had not been canonized as "Torah"—literally "Teaching" in the broadest sense—and if "Torah" in turn, had not constantly renewed itself as "Tradition."

FIRST TEXT:

Moses received Torah from Sinai and delivered it to Joshua and Joshua to the Elders, and the Elders to the Prophets and the Prophets delivered it to the Men of the Great Synagogue.

Thus the opening of the Mishnah *Avot,* declaring the Pharisaic "Chain of Tradition" *(Shalshelet ha-qabbalah)* which would ultimately stretch through the Talmudic period down to the end of the Middle Ages. Laconic though it be, the passage seems to me to capture the essence of collective memory as a dual movement of reception and transmission, successively propelling itself toward the future. It is this process which forges the *mneme* of the group, the continuum of its memory, which is that of the links in a chain and not that of a silken thread. The Jews were not mnemonic virtuosos. They were, however, willing receivers and superb transmitters.

SECOND TEXT (Babylonian Talmud, tractate *Shabbat* 138a):

When our Masters entered the Vineyard at Yabneh they said: The Torah is destined to be forgotten in Israel, as it is written (Amos 8:11) *Behold the days come, says the Lord God, that I will send a famine in the land, not a famine of bread nor a thirst for water, but of hearing the words of the Lord.*

The somber passage is unexpected, almost shocking. It cannot be explained merely as an inevitable exegesis of the biblical verse it cites. The key to understanding lies in the time and place in which the tradition itself has set these words. The "Vineyard at Yabneh" refers to the academy established by Rabbi Yochanan ben Zakkai when the Second Temple, that most pivotal of all Jewish places of memory, was destroyed by the Romans. Yabneh was the fortress against oblivion. It was there that the tradition was salvaged, studied, and recast in forms that insured its continuity for ages to come. I know of nothing that epitomizes the enduring power of Yabneh more vividly than the fact that while Freud the psychologist rejected the "chain of tradition" in favor of the chain of unconscious repetition, Freud the Jew still understood and felt the meaning of that remote event. In August 1938, having fled his Viennese Jerusalem in the wake of the *Anschluss,* he instinctively reaches back to Yabneh for a transparent parable of consolation which he sends through Anna Freud to the psychoanalytic diaspora assembled in Paris for the Fifteenth International Congress:

> The political misfortune of the [Jewish] nation taught them to appreciate the only possession they had retained, their Scripture, at its true value. Immediately after the destruction of the Temple by Titus, Rabbi Yochanan ben Zakkai asked for permission to open at Yabneh the first school for the study of the Torah. From now on it was the Holy Book and the intellectual effort applied to it that kept the people together.[7]

Just so. It seems therefore all the more strange that the dire prediction that the Torah will be forgotten should have been made by those who laid the foundations for its future transmission. But they, of course, could not have known how lasting their work would be. What we have here is not so much a prediction as a projection of their own present anxiety that the Torah is in peril of oblivion. What, then, is Torah for the sages of Yabneh? The Teaching, after all, includes a large measure of history as well. However, as the subsequent discussion immediately reveals, the specific anxiety here is not that "history" but the *halakhah,* the Law, may be forgotten. The priorities are clear; it is the *halakhah* that is primary. And indeed, only the history that was relevant to the value system of the *halakhah* was remembered. The rest was ignored, "forgotten."

THIRD TEXT (Babylonian Talmud, tractate *Sukkah* 20a):

. . . in ancient times when the Torah was forgotten from Israel, Ezra came up from Babylon and established it. [Some of it] was again forgotten and Hillel the Babylonian came up and established it. Yet again was [some of it] forgotten, and R. Hiyya and his sons came up and established it.

So the tradition also knows of three occasions when the Torah was, in whole or in part, actually forgotten and then restored. The general sense is evident. That which the people has "forgotten" can, under certain circumstances, be retrieved. The first of the three examples is the best known and the most significant. In the eighth chapter of the Book of Nehemiah, Ezra assembles the people before the Water Gate in Jerusalem for what may be called a dramatic exercise in national recollection. But as in any collective anamnesis, what is retrieved is also metamorphosed. For the first time, during the seven days of Tabernacles, Ezra and his associates read aloud the entire text of the Torah—here the term refers to the Five Books of Moses—as one continuous "book" *(sefer),* publicly, before the whole people, while the Levites expound its meaning. That is to say, for the first time in history the sacred text becomes the common property of a people and not merely of its priests. Thus is Scripture born. Thus exegesis is born. Thus the religion of ancient Israel becomes Judaism and Yabneh becomes possible.

V

We are not assembled at the Water Gate, but at Royaumont, and I shall not weary you further with ancient texts. I have brought these before you to serve as paradigms, incomplete, to be sure, for the functioning of collective memory; for a crisis of forgetting; for collective anamnesis—all within a specific tradition in which the problem of memory and forgetting has always occupied a privileged place. Our texts are limited; they cannot possibly cover the entire terrain of forgetting. Clearly there was a kind of forgetting that, by its very nature, is never mentioned in the sources, for there were things, even mighty things, that were truly and completely *forgotten*. To take but one example: as monotheism became rooted in ancient Israel the entire rich and awesome world of pagan Near Eastern mythology was suppressed and forgotten so that all that was remembered was its prophetic caricature as mere idolatry, the worship of inanimate figures of wood and stone.

Our texts are paradigmatic, I submit, because the issues they raise transcend their Jewish contexts, because the phenomenology of collective memory and forgetting is essentially the same for all social groups, though the details may vary widely. For any people there are certain fundamental elements of the past—historical or mythic, often a fusion of both—that become "Torah," be it oral or written, a teaching that is canonical, shared, commanding consensus; and only insofar as this "Torah" becomes "tradition" does it survive. Every group, every people, has its *halakhah,* for *halakhah* is not "Law," *nomos,* in the Alexandrian, let alone the Pauline, sense. The Hebrew noun derives from *halakh,* "to walk," hence *halakhah*—the Path on which one walks, the Way, the "Tao"—the complex of rites and beliefs that gives a people its sense of identity and purpose. Only those moments out of the past are transmitted that are felt to be formative or exemplary for the *halakhah* of a people as it is lived in the present; the rest of "history" falls, one might almost say literally, by the "wayside."

And, at certain junctures, peoples are also capable of anamnesis, though it is not the group as such that initiates the process, but outstanding individuals or elites—Ezras and Levites, if you wish. Every "renaissance," every "reformation," reaches back into an often distant past to recover forgotten or neglected elements with which there is a sudden sympathetic vibration, a sense of empathy, of recognition. Inevitably, every such anamnesis also transforms the recovered past into something new; inexorably, it denigrates the intermediate past as something that deserves to be forgotten. In any case, if the achievement is not to be ephemeral, it must itself become a tradition, with all that this entails.

Though modern historiography may give the illusion of both *mneme* and *anamnesis,* it is really neither collective memory nor recollection in any of their prior senses, but a radically new venture. The past it constantly recreates is often barely recognizable to what remains of collective memory; the past it retrieves is indeed a lost past, but it is not the one we feel we have lost. I have written of this sufficiently in *Zakhor* and need not elaborate here.

The detachment of the modern historian from the group and its memory did not occur immediately. The historian in the nineteenth century begins his work still rooted in the organic life of his people and in a shared pan-European culture, as a molder, refiner, and restorer of memory. More than a scholar and writer of history, he feels himself, with some justification, an actor in history. But along the way he also discovers that through his methods he is capable of an *anamnesis* far beyond what the group can even conceive. The entire past has become accessible to his modes of inquiry, and the quest for this total past cannot be resisted. At the same time, his growing desire for scientific objectivity seems to demand that he distance himself ever more from the living concerns of the group and, indeed, from his own subject matter. Both tendencies now seem, in retrospect, almost inevitable. Thus history becomes a discipline with an independent, ever accelerating momentum, until Nietzsche diagnoses a malignancy. What began as a cure has become the illness. And he is only the first of many to see it as such.

The problem with which we began—how much to remember and how much to forget—can never be answered from within the discipline itself, for it is not memory with which it is concerned. This does not mean that modern historiography is not selective, only that its principles of selectivity are internal—the state of the field, the coherence of the argument, the structure of the presentation. In principle, however, from the same inner perspective of the discipline, no aspect of the past, down to its most arcane details, is unworthy of research and publication. And that, of course, is how it should be. For if it is knowledge of the past that we seek, who is to decide *a priori* which fact is not potentially valuable? What working historian has not found in some dry and obscure monograph the tiny but vital link that he needed in order to pursue a larger theme? For the historian God, indeed, dwells in the details, though memory protests that the details have become gods. There is no way out of this impasse, for the issue lies elsewhere.

Our real problem is that we are without a *halakhah.* Like Kafka's man from the country, we yearn for the Law, but it is no longer accessible to us. What has long been called the crisis of historicism is but a reflection of the crisis of our culture, of our spiritual life. If there be a malignancy, its source lies not in the historical quest, but in the loss of a *halakhah* that will know what to appropriate and what to leave behind, a commonality of values that would enable us to transform history into memory. This the historian alone cannot accomplish. He can, indeed, write an as yet unwritten history of forgetting—had I so chosen I could have brought a small chapter before you today—but he cannot tell us what should be forgotten, for that is the prerogative of *halakhah.*

Dissonant Epilogue

At this late point I pause—abruptly—wondering why I have had such unusual difficulty writing this paper, why it has been such a constant struggle. The pressure of time, the transition from New York to Paris are not sufficient to explain it. As I have done so many times, I repeat to myself the title of this conference and then, suddenly, I believe I know why. I take the risk of telling it to you publicly.

"The Uses of Forgetting." The title is charming, tantalizing with its touch of paradox, a bit precious perhaps, certainly original. But I realize too late that something deep within me has been rebelling against this title all along. An inner voice whispers: Can you imagine such a conference in Prague, or in Santiago de Chile? . . . And to my dismay I begin to wonder whether, unwittingly and indirectly, I myself may not have contributed to the emergence of this very theme which now arouses my strongest resistance.

Toward the end of *Zakhor* I appropriated Jorge Luis Borges's *Funes el memorioso*—the fictional brother of Luria's mnemonist—as a parable for the excesses of modern historiography. I have since become aware that, perhaps because of this parable, some readers have interpreted the entire book as a rejection on my part of the historical enterprise *per se,* or as a nostalgia for premodern modes of historical cognition. I, of course, intended nothing of the sort, and was careful to say so explicitly. My purpose in *Zakhor* was to make a sharp distinction between collective memory and historiography, and, certainly, to underscore the hypertrophy of the latter. I retract none of this. But at a conference entitled "Usages de l'oubli" I must add this postscript for the sake of clarity.

Historiography, I will continue to insist, cannot be a substitute for collective memory, nor does it show signs of creating an alternative tradition that is capable of being shared. But the essential dignity of the historical vocation remains, and its moral imperative seems to me now more urgent than ever. For in the world in which we live it is no longer merely a question of the decay of collective memory and the declining consciousness of the past, but of the aggressive rape of whatever memory remains, the deliberate distortion of the historical record, the invention of mythological pasts in the service of the powers of darkness. Against the agents of oblivion, the shredders of documents, the assassins of memory, the revisers of encyclopedias, the conspirators of silence, against those who, in Kundera's wonderful image, can airbrush a man out of a photograph so that nothing is left of him but his hat—only the historian, with the austere passion for fact, proof, evidence, which are central to his vocation, can effectively stand guard.

And so, given that we cannot draw the lines between too much and too little historical research, for we have no *halakhah* beyond ourselves. If this be the choice, I will take my stand on the side of "too much" rather than "too little," for my terror of forgetting is greater than my terror of having too much to remember. Let the accumulated facts about the past continue to multiply. Let the flood of books and monographs grow, even if they are only read by specialists. Let unread copies lie on the shelves of many libraries, so that if some be destroyed or removed others will remain. So that those who need can find that this person did live, those events really took place, this interpretation is not the only one. So that those who may someday forge a new *halakhah* may sift and retrieve what they require.

Shortly before I left New York my friend Pierre Birnbaum sent me a page from *Le Monde* reporting a poll it had conducted as to whether Klaus Barbie should be put on trial. The central question was formulated as follows: "Des deux mots suivants, *oubli* ou *justice,* quel est celui qui charactérise le mieux votre attitude face aux événements de cette période de la guerre et de l'Occupation?" (Of the two following words, *forgetting* or *justice,* which is the one that best characterizes your attitude toward the events of this period of the war and the Occupation?)[8]

Can it be that the journalists have stumbled across something more important than they perhaps realized? Is it possible that the antonym of "forgetting" is not "remembering," but *justice?*

My reflections were jotted down restlessly and in solitude. Perhaps they are far from the vision of those who planned this conference. If so, may the Angel of Forgetfulness come to you quickly.

Notes

ABBREVIATIONS

HUCA	Hebrew Union College Annual
JQR	Jewish Quarterly Review
MGWJ	Monatsschrift für Geschichte und Wissenschaft des Judentums
MJC	Medievel Jewish Chronicles, ed. A. Neubauer
n.d.	no date of printing
n.p.	no place of printing
o.s.	old series
PAAJR	Proceedings of the American Academy for Jewish Research
REJ	Revue des études juives
TB	Babylonian Talmud
TP	Palestinian Talmud

PREFACE

1. Published as *Mémoire et Histoire, données et débats. Actes du XXVe Colloque des intellectuels juifs de langue française* (Paris, 1986). My own contribution, "Vers une histoire de l'espoir juif" (*ibid.*, pp. 91–107), appeared earlier in *Esprit,* no. 104–105 (Aug.–Sept. 1985), pp. 24–38.

2. Pierre Nora (ed.), *Les lieux de mémoire*, I: *La République*; II–IV: *La Nation* (Paris, 1984 et seq.).

3. See his introductory essay to vol. I, entitled "Entre Mémoire et Histoire: la problématique des lieux."

4. *Usages de l'oubli: Contributions . . . au Colloque de Royaumont* (Paris, 1988).

1. BIBLICAL AND RABBINIC FOUNDATIONS

1. The meaning and functions of this verb are amply discussed in the complementary studies of B. S. Childs, *Memory and Tradition in Israel* (London, 1962), and W. Schottroff, *'Gedenken' im alten Orient und im Alten Testament: Die Wurzel zäkar im Semitischen Sprachkreis* (Neukirchen-Vluyn, 1964). Cf. also P. A. H. de Boer, *Gedenken und Gedächtnis in der Welt des Alten Testaments* (Stuttgart, 1962). The covenant relationship in the Bible demands that not only Israel must "remember," but God as well. Indeed, He can be challenged and even upbraided for having "forgotten"; for a particularly vivid example of this, see Psalm 44. Needless to say, these lectures attempt to deal only with the human side of the equation.

2. See especially M. Eliade, *The Myth of the Eternal Return* (New York, 1954), pp. 34–48 and *passim*. The periodic abolition of historical time through myth and ritual is a consistent and major theme throughout Eliade's works, e.g.: *The Sacred and the Profane* (New York, 1959), ch. 2; *Myths, Dreams and Mysteries* (New York, 1960), ch. 3; *Myth and Reality* (New York, 1968), chs. 5–6; *Yoga: Immortality and Freedom* (New York, 1958), pp. 39–40. Eliade's phenomenological analysis, based on an impressive array of comparative materials, persuades. However, his far-reaching historical and philosophical conclusions, in which the mythic abolition of history is extolled as salvation from the "terror of history," leap well beyond the evidence. See the brief but cogent remarks of R. J. Zwi Werblowsky in his review of the first of the aforementioned works in *Journal of Jewish Studies*, 6 (1955):172–75.

3. R. C. Majumdar, "Ideas of History in Sanskrit Literature," in *Historians of India, Pakistan and Ceylon*, ed. C. H. Philips (London, 1961), p. 25. Cf. K. Quecke, "Der indische Geist und die Geschichte," *Saeculum*, 1 (1950):362–79, who opens with the sweeping assertion that "kein anderes Kulturvolk der Menschheit hat eine solch unvorstellbare Gleichgültigkeit gegenüber der Wahrheit historischer Tatsachen bewiesen wie die Inder." The great Far-Eastern contrast to India in this respect is, of course, China, whose prodigious historiographical achievement is only gradually being recognized by Western scholars. A significant effort to bridge the gap is the collaborative volume on *Historians of China and Japan*, ed. W. G. Beasley and E. G. Pulleyblank (London, 1961). On Chinese attitudes, not merely to historical writing but to time and history generally, see Joseph Needham's splendid essay on "Time and Knowledge in China and the West," in *The Voices of Time*, ed. J. T. Fraser (New York, 1966), pp. 92–135.

4. I use "meaning in history" here solely in the sense of a transcendent meaning, and do not suggest thereby that without it, as in Greece (or China), history is necessarily meaningless. Nor is it my intent to endorse

any of the rigid distinctions that are often posited between Hebrew and Greek ways of thinking, in particular their alleged radically contrasting modes of perceiving time. For examples of the latter position, see O. Cullman, *Christ and Time* (London, 1951); J. Marsh, *The Fullness of Time* (London, 1952); T. Bowman, *Hebrew Thought Compared with Greek* (London, 1960); and the sharp critiques of J. Barr, *Biblical Words for Time* (2nd rev. ed.; London, 1969), arguing that biblical thought and attitudes cannot be elicited from its lexical stock or linguistic structures, and A. Momigliano, "Time in Ancient Historiography," *History and Theory*, Beiheft 6 (1966):1–23 (reprinted in his *Essays in Ancient and Modern Historiography* [Middletown Conn., 1977], pp. 179–204). Nevertheless, perceptions of time and views of history constitute two separate issues. Whatever the case with regard to the actual experience of time, conceptions of history in ancient Israel and Greece were, on other grounds, demonstrably different. On the specific question of linear vs. cyclical time, see below, note 7.

5. This does not mean that archetypal *thinking* disappeared, only that the archetypal events were now located within history rather than in a primeval mythic time. The exodus from Egypt is the outstanding example of such an historical archetype, serving as a pattern for the narrative of the crossing of the Jordan, visions of the messianic redemption, and much besides. Exodus typology has been widely discussed in biblical scholarship. For its possible legal and social analogues, see D. Daube, *The Exodus Pattern in the Bible* (All Souls Studies, vol. 2, London, 1963). The tendency to assimilate new events to central events of the past was greatly intensified in rabbinic thinking, and remained characteristic thereafter. For its effects on Jewish perceptions of history in the Middle Ages, see lecture 2.

6. For a concise and lucid discussion of biblical "theology" as historical recital, see G. E. Wright, *God Who Acts* (London, 1952). The essential point was grasped already in the twelfth century by Judah Halevi. See the speech of the Rabbi, contrasted with that of the Philosopher, in Halevi's *Kuzari*, trans. H. Hirschfeld (New York, 1946), p. 41.

7. I have phrased the matter thus, fully aware of various attempts to discern cyclical notions of one kind or another in biblical historiography. See most recently G. W. Trompf, *The Idea of Recurrence in Western Thought: From Antiquity to the Renaissance* (Berkeley, 1979); on the Hebrew scriptures, see pp. 116–20, 134–39, 156–64. Such efforts may be regarded as reactions to prevalent oversimplistic views concerning the "linear" character of Hebrew thinking about history as opposed to the "cyclical" thinking of the Greeks. Certainly both generalizations are in need of correction. To focus only on the former, if the Hebrew conception of history is "linear," the line is surely not an unbroken one, nor is it an ever-ascending curve of progress. Still, I find it hard to grasp how

Trompf's broadening of the notion of cycle to include such paradigms as "alternation," "re-enactment," "renovation, restoration and Renaissance," advances our understanding, or whether the term "recurrence" (used instead of "cycle" to avoid the implication of a literal repetition of events) can embrace these and other disparate phenomena without ultimately misleading. Another paradigm, which Trompf styles "the reciprocal view," also serves him as a prime example of biblical recurrence. He defines it as "the view that common types of events are followed by consequences in such a way as to exemplify a general pattern in history." When to these criteria are added "belief in the uniformity of human nature," "preoccupation with parallelism," and, "connected with almost all the above . . . the view that the past teaches lessons for present and future action," one wonders if there has ever been any kind of historiography prior to modern times from which, by such definitions, one could not extract an idea of "recurrence." If so, however, the term has been stretched to the bursting point and is no longer valuable.

Significantly, Trompf is himself somewhat uneasy about abandoning the "linear" model altogether. He readily concedes that once eschatology took hold in Israel there was no room for real doctrines of recurrence. But even apart from this "the ancient Hebrews and early Christians were clearly opposed to the belief in an eternal return. Admittedly, the Israelites participated in yearly festivals, and they could speak of the 'return,' the 'coming around,' or the 'circuit' of seasons and natural events. But it is remarkable how they still managed to think historically when, for their immediate neighbors at any rate, human life was under the flux of 'unhistorical, cyclically oriented nature mythologies and the magical ordinances of fate' [quoting V. Hamp]. . . . To this extent at least, then, the Judeo-Christian–linear/Greek–cyclical contrast still has worth" (Trompf 1979: 118ff.).

8. This "Credo . . . bears all the marks of great antiquity" (G. Von Rad, *Old Testament Theology* (New York, 1961) 1:121. Cf. also the somewhat more elaborate declaration in Josh. 24:2–14.

9. Yehezkel Kaufmann, *Toledot ha-'emunah ha-Yisraelit* [History of Israelite religion] (2nd ed.; Jerusalem-Tel Aviv, 1954), 1 (Book 1): 190–94; 2 (Book 1):378ff.; and, in greater detail, *The Biblical Account of the Conquest of Palestine*, trans. M. Dagut (Jerusalem, 1954), especially pp. 46–56.

10. Von Rad has effectively stated the essential point: "Historical poetry was the form in which Israel, like other peoples, made sure of historical facts. That is, of their location and their significance. In those times poetry was, as a rule, the one possible form for expressing basic insights. It was not just there along with prose as something one might elect to use—a more elevated form of discourse as it were—but poetry alone enabled a people to express experiences met with in the course of

their history in such a way as to make the past become absolutely present. In the case of legend we now know that we must reckon with this co-efficient of interpretation. But in thinking of the literary stories, which extend from the Hexateuch to II Kings, and which we must also regard to begin with as poetry, we have to learn to grasp this coefficient more clearly in its special features in any given story. . . . The understanding of lists and annals is independent of the presuppositions of faith. But these poetic stories appeal for assent; they address those who are prepared to ask questions and receive answers along like lines. . . ." (*Old Testament Theology*, 1:109).

11. The relationship between the two remains problematic. Reflecting a widespread assumption, Momigliano writes: "The Hebrew historian never claimed to be a prophet. He never said 'the spirit of the Lord is upon me.' But the pages of the historical books of the Bible are full of prophets who interpret the events because they know what was, is and will be. The historian by implication subordinates himself to the prophet; he derives his values from him" (*Essays in Ancient and Modern Historiography*, p. 195). It is striking, however, that with the sole exception of Isaiah, none of the classical prophets is even mentioned by the biblical historians. More significantly, throughout the historical literature from Deuteronomy through II Kings, national catastrophe is always related to religious and cultic sins and not, as was the primary message of classical prophecy from Amos on, to social and moral evils. See Kaufmann, *Toledot*, 1 (1):25–31. Kaufmann's view that Hebrew historiography and prophecy represent independent developments out of a common ground in Israelite monotheism impresses me as essentially correct.

12. E.g., such lost works as the "Book of the Acts of Solomon" (I Kings 11:41) and the books of the "Chronicles" of the Kings of Judah and of Israel (I Kings 1:18 and 14:19, respectively, and often thereafter).

13. On Hellenistic Jewish historical writings of which, with the exception of Maccabees I-III, only quoted fragments survive, see E. Schürer, *Geschichte des jüdischen Volkes im Zeitalter Jesu Christi* (Leipzig, 1901–11), 3:468–97; R. H. Pfeiffer, *History of New Testament Times, with an Introduction to the Apocrypha* (New York, 1949), pp. 200–6; Y. Gutman, *Ha-sifrut ha-Yehudit ha-Hellenistit* [Jewish-Hellenistic Literature], 1 (Jerusalem, 1958):132–39, and 2 (Jerusalem, 1963):73–143.

14. It should be recognized that this fixed and perpetual public reading of the Scriptures had, simultaneously, dual consequences. The ritualized repetition of the readings, whether annual or triennial, endowed even the historical narratives with a certain cyclical quality. I return to this point in lecture 2.

15. I refer to Joseph ben Joshua Ha-Kohen of Avignon, on whom see lecture 3.

16. See *Bereshit Rabbah* 3:5 and 9:2 (ed. J. Theodor and Ch. Albeck [reprint Jerusalem, 1965], 1:23, 68, and the parallel passages cited there).

17. In the Bible see, for example Is. 27:1, 51:9; Ps. 74:13–14, 89:11; Job 9:13, 26:12–13. Contrast, in rabbinic literature, TB *Baba Bathra* 74b; *Shemot Rabbah* 15:22; *Bamidbar Rabbah* 18:22, 21:18; *Tanhuma* Ḥukkat 1. Cf. also TB *Ḥagigah* 12a.

18. Louis Ginzberg, *The Legends of the Jews*, 7 vols. (Philadelphia, 1909–38).

19. The problem had already begun to be recognized in the late nineteenth century. Thus, for example, Israel Lévi could write: "Que de mal se sont donné les savants, depuis Krochmal jusqu'à notre regretté maître Joseph Derenbourg, pour découvrir dans les sources talmudiques des renseignements sur l'histoire juive avant l'ère chrétienne, et que restera-t-il un jour de ce labeur prodigieux! Quand on reprend froidement tous ces textes sur lesquels on a cru pouvoir edifier des constructions historiques, on est tout surpris d'en reconnaître la fragilité: ce sont tres souvent de simples *aggadot*, des anecdotes imaginées de toutes pièces en vue de l'edification ou même de l'amusement des lecteurs . . ." ("Les sources talmudiques de l'histoire juive," *REJ*, 35 (1897):213. For a broader view of the issues, see J. Neusner, "The Religious Uses of History: Judaism in First Century A.D. Palestine and Third Century Babylonia," *History and Theory*, 5 (1966):154. Structured specifically around the rabbinic responses to the destruction of the Second Temple and to the rise of the Sassanians, Neusner's essay formulates and elucidates some central problems in the rabbinic attitude toward history generally.

20. The most valuable attempt to analyze the rabbinic understanding of history on its own terms, rather than to judge it by alien standards, is still N. N. Glatzer's *Untersuchungen zur Geschichtslehre der Tannaiten* (Berlin, 1933).

21. E.g., *Bereshit Rabbah* 46:4: "R. Huna declared in the name of Bar Kappara: Abraham sat and deduced a *gezerah shavah* [i.e., an analogy between two laws based on a verbal congruence; one of the logical modes of rabbinic hermeneutics].... R. Hanina bar Pazi said to him: 'And were *gezerot shavot*, then, already given to Abraham?!'" See also *ibid.* 63:7 [after it has been implied, on the basis of Gen. 25:22, that Rebekah went to houses of study]: "And were there, then, synagogues and houses of study in those days?"

22. TB *Menahot* 29b (my italics).

23. The formulation in TP *Pe'ah* 17:1 is particularly apposite here:

"All that a mature disciple will yet expound before his master has already been told to Moses at Sinai."

24. Significant attempts to uncover the latent structures of rabbinic thought will be found in M. Kadushin's *Organic Thinking* (New York, 1938), and *The Rabbinic Mind* (New York, 1952). For the processes of aggadic interpretation in particular, the most valuable and comprehensive work is that of Y. Heinemann, *Darkey ha-'aggadah* [The methods of the Aggadah] (Jerusalem, 1940; 2nd ed., 1954). The striking similarities between certain hermeneutical rules of the rabbis in interpreting the Bible, and those of the Alexandrian grammarians in interpreting Homer and Hesiod, were brought into sharp relief by S. Lieberman in his *Hellenism in Jewish Palestine* (New York 1950); see pp. 47–82, "Rabbinic Interpretation of Scripture."

25. The original Aramaic text, along with the much later Hebrew scholia, has been edited several times. See A. Neubauer, *MJC*, 2:3–25; S. Zeitlin, *Megillat Taanit as a Source for Jewish Chronology and History in the Hellenistic and Roman Periods* (Philadelphia, 1922); H. Lichtenstein, "Die Fastenrolle: Untersuchung zur Jüdisch-Hellenistischen Geschichte," *HUCA*, 8–9 (1931–32):257–351 (the fundamental study); and, most recently, B. Z. Lurie, *Megillat Ta'anit*, with Hebrew introduction and commentary (Jerusalem, 1964). Not surprisingly, although it is Lurie's goal to examine the work as an historical *source* for the Hasmonean period, he characterizes it as "unique in its form in our *ancient historical literature*" (p. 9, my italics).

26. Conventionally designated as *Seder 'Olam Rabba* [The Greater Order of the World] merely to distinguish it from the so-called *Seder 'Olam Zuta*, or "Minor Order," which is a later Geonic work. The text has been edited by Neubauer, *MJC*, 2:26–67, and by B. Ratner (Vilna 1897). An edition with German translation published by A. Marx (Berlin, 1903) covers only the first ten chapters and was never completed.

27. An extreme and relatively recent instance of this may be found in B. Dinur, "Ha-fragmentim ha-histori'im be-sifrut ha-Talmud u-ba'ayot ha-heker bahem" [Historiographical fragments in Talmudic literature and the problems of their investigation] in *Proceedings of the Fifth World Congress of Jewish Studies* (1969) (Jerusalem, 1972), vol. 2 [Hebrew section], pp. 137–46, with English abstract [English section], pp. 251–52.

28. "Since the deaths of Haggai, Zachariah and Malachi, the Holy Spirit has ceased in Israel" (Tosefta *Sotah* 13; TB *Sotah* 48b, *Yoma* 9b, *Sanhedrin* 11a. Cf. *Seder 'Olam Rabbah*, ch. 30 (ed. Neubauer, p. 65): "*And the rough he-goat is the King of Greece* [Dan. 7:21]—that is, Alexander of Macedon. Up to this point the prophets were prophesying through the Holy Spirit; from this point on, incline thine ear and hearken unto the words of the sages." Such, at least, was the accepted scheme. In

reality another type of "prophecy," crystallized in the apocalyptic literature, continued unabated.

29. The *locus classicus* is TB *Yoma* 9b: "Why was the First Temple destroyed? Because of three things which prevailed there: idolatry, immorality, bloodshed. . . . But why was the Second Temple destroyed, seeing that in its time they were occupying themselves with Torah, precepts, and the practice of charity? Because therein prevailed hatred without cause."

30. *Vayyikra Rabbah* 29:2. The number of rungs signifies years of domination over Israel. The eagle is interpreted, appropriately, as a symbol of Rome.

31. TB *Sanhedrin* 98a. For further variations on this theme, see A. Berger, "Captive at the Gate of Rome: The Story of a Messianic Motif," *PAAJR*, 44 (1977):1–17.

32. That there was no rabbinic conspiracy to obliterate the memory of the Hasmonean dynasty was argued vigorously by G. Alon, "Ha-hishkihah ha-'umah va-hakhameha 'et ha-Hashmona'im?" [Did the nation and its sages cause the Hasmoneans to be forgotten?], reprinted in his *Mehqarim be-toledot Yisrael* [Studies in Jewish history] (Jerusalem, 1967), 1:15–25. Be that as it may, even if the rabbis did not deliberately suppress the history of the Hasmoneans, it remains a fact that they made no special effort to preserve or record it.

33. See A. H. Silver's schematic survey in *A History of Messianic Speculation in Israel* (reprint, Boston, 1959), Part II ("Opposition to Messianic Speculation"), pp. 195–239, and especially G. Scholem, "Toward an Understanding of the Messianic Idea," in *The Messianic Idea in Judaism and Other Essays on Jewish Spirituality* (New York, 1971), pp. 1–36.

34. TB *Sanhedrin* 97b.

35. It need hardly be added that much of what is related of Alexander Jannaeus in rabbinic literature is unhistorical. For a review of the rabbinic sources, see B. Lurie, *Yannai ha-melekh* (Jerusalem, 1960), and his *Mi-Yannai 'ad Hurdus* (Jerusalem, 1974), especially chs. 14–18.

36. See L. Ginzberg, "The Mishnah *Tamid*," *Journal of Jewish Lore and Philosophy*, 1 (1919):33–44, 197–209, 265–95.

37. It is characteristic, again, that although the martyrdom of Jewish scholars at the hands of the Romans is certainly historical, the traditions are problematic and the details full of aggadic embellishments. See L. Finkelstein, "The Ten Martyrs," *Essays and Studies in Memory of Linda R. Miller* (New York, 1938), pp. 29–55; and cf. S. Lieberman, "The Martyrs of Caesaria," *Annuaire de l'Institut de Philologie et d'Histoire Orientales et Slaves*, 7 (1939–44), especially pp. 416 ff.

38. A lingering uneasiness at the source of authority for the blessing is still perceptible in TB *Shabbat* 23a: "What benediction is uttered?

This: 'Who sanctified us by His commandments and commanded us to kindle the light of Hanukkah.' And where did He command us? Rabbi Awiya said: [It follows from] *thou shalt not turn aside [from the sentence which he shall show thee]* (Deut. 17:11). Rabbi Nahman quoted: *Ask they father and he shall show thee; thine elders, and they will tell thee* (Deut. 32:7). Cf. also *Midrash Tehillim* 22:10: "R. Benjamin bar Japheth taught in the name of R. Eleazar: 'As the dawn ends the night, so all the miracles ended with Esther.' But what of Hanukkah? We speak, however, only of the miracles which are recorded in Scripture."

2. THE MIDDLE AGES

1. A claim for actual "epochs of historical creativity" among medieval Jews was made by H. H. Ben-Sasson, "Li-megamot ha-kronografiah ha-Yehudit shel yemey ha-benayim" [Trends in the Jewish chronography of the Middle Ages], published in *Historionim ve-'askolot historiot* [Historians and historical schools: The seventh convention of the Historical Society of Israel] (Jerusalem, 1962), pp. 29–49. I have criticized this view in my "Clio and the Jews," *American Academy for Jewish Research Jubilee Volume* (=*PAAJR*, 46–47, 1978–79), 2 (1980):615.

2. On Jewish histories of tradition and their Muslim parallels see the introduction of G. D. Cohen to his critical edition and English translation of Abraham Ibn Daud's *Sefer Ha-Qabbalah: The Book of Tradition* (Philadelphia, 1967), pp. 50–57. The classical "chain of tradition" is to be found, of course, in the first chapter of Mishnah *Abot*. For similar Greek sequences and their possible influence, see E. Bickerman, "La chaine de la tradition pharisienne," *Revue Biblique*, 59 (1952):44–54.

3. See the introduction to Sherira's *Iggeret*, ed. B. M. Lewin (Haifa, 1921; reprinted Jerusalem, 1972), pp. 5–6.

4. Maimonides, *Epistle to Yemen*, Judeo-Arabic text and three medieval Hebrew translations, ed. A. S. Halkin, English trans. B. Cohen (New York, 1952), pp. xviii–xx.

5. Maimonides, *Commentary to Mishnah Sanhedrin*, 10:1. Cf. *Guide of the Perplexed* (Moreh Nebukhim), 1,1, trans. S. Pines (Chicago, 1963), 1:24. In the introduction to his Mishnah commentary he even speaks slightingly concerning the importance of the chain of tradition itself, which has "no great use for belief in the Lord," but may be studied by anyone "who desires to be complete in his study of Mishnah." On Maimonides and Arabic historiography, see S. W. Baron, "The Historical Outlook of Maimonides," *PAAJR*, 6 (1935), reprinted in his *History and Jewish Historians* (Philadelphia, 1964), especially pp. 110–14.

Nevertheless, Maimonides had his own historical interests and sensitivities. For the significance and impact of his tendency to "historicize" certain biblical laws as having been ordained in order to wean the ancient Israelites away from the pagan ("Sabaean") practices of their time, see A. Funkenstein, "Gesetz und Geschichte: Zur historisierenden Hermeneutik bei Maimonides und Thomas von Aquin," *Viator*, 1 (1970):147–78; and cf. now I. Twersky, *Introduction to the Code of Maimonides* (New Haven, 1980), pp. 220–28, 389ff.

6. Moses Ibn Ezra, *Kitab al-Muhadara wal-Mudhakara*, ed. with Hebrew trans. by A. S. Halkin (Jerusalem, 1975), pp. 50–51.

7. Solomon Ibn Verga, *Shebet Yehudah*, ed. A. Shohat, intro. by Y. Baer (Jerusalem, 1947), p. 21.

8. For such works up to the thirteenth century see the survey of S. W. Baron, *A Social and Religious History of the Jews* (2nd rev. ed.; New York, 1952—in progress), 6:188–234. (The discussion is aptly placed within a chapter entitled "Homilies and Histories.")

9. Now available in D. Flusser's critical edition, *Sefer Yosippon*, 2 vols. (Jerusalem, 1978–80).

10. First published in *Ozar Tob* [supplement to *Magazin für die Wissenschaft des Judenthums*] (Berlin, 1877–78), pp. 17–18. Reprinted in *Sefer Yosippon*, ed. H. Hominer (Jerusalem, 1965), p. 37.

11. Reprinted by Hominer, *ibid.*, p. 41.

12. Out of the rather extensive literature on the book and its anonymous author, see especially: Y. Baer, "Sefer Yosippon ha-'ibri," in *Sefer Dinaburg* (Jerusalem, 1949), pp. 128–205; D. Flusser, "Mehaber Sefer Yosippon: Demuto u-tequfato" [The author of Yosippon: His image and his time], *Zion*, 18 (1953):109–26; *idem*, "Mehaber Sefer ha-Yosippon ke-historion" [The author of Yosippon as an historian], in *Meqomam shel toledot 'Am Yisrael be-misgeret toledot ha-'amim* [The place of Jewish history within the history of the nations: the sixteenth convention of the Historical Society of Israel] (Jerusalem, 1973), pp. 203–26; *idem*, *Sefer Yosippon*, vol. 2.

13. *Sefer Yosippon*, ed. Hominer, p. 43.

14. S. Kraus, "Ha-shemot Ashkenaz u-Sefarad" [The names 'Ashkenaz' and 'Sefarad'], *Tarbiz*, 3 (1931–32):423–35; *idem*, "Die Hebräischen Bennenungen der modernen Völker," *Jewish Studies in Memory of George A. Kohut* (New York, 1935), pp. 379–412. Cf. also A. I. Laredo and D. G. Maeso, "El nombre de 'Sefarad'," *Sefarad*, 4 (1944):349–63.

15. Rich materials will be found in the anthologies of Y. Eben-Shemuel, *Midreshey ge'ulah* [Jewish apocalyptic texts from the sixth to the thirteenth centuries] (2nd ed.; Jerusalem–Tel Aviv, 1954), and A. Z. Aescoly, *Ha-tenu'ot ha-meshihiot be-Yisrael* [Jewish messianic movements, from the Bar-Kokhba revolt to the expulsion of the Jews from Spain] (Jerusalem, 1956).

16. All four Hebrew Crusade chronicles were edited by A. Neubauer and M. Stern, with German translation by S. Baer, as *Hebräische Berichte über die Judenverfolgungen während der Kreuzzuge* (Quellen zur Geschichte der Juden in Deutschland, vol. 2, Berlin, 1892), and by A. M. Habermann in his *Sefer gezerot Ashkenaz ve-Zarefat* [The book of the persecutions of Germany and France] (Jerusalem, 1945). An English translation is now available by S. Eidelberg, *The Jews and the Crusaders: The Hebrew Chronicles of the First and Second Crusades* (Madison, Wisconsin, 1977).

17. On the decline of Babylonia and the rise of new centers, albeit couched in legendary form, see *Sefer Ha-Qabbalah*, ed. G. D. Cohen, pp. 46ff. (Hebrew), pp. 63ff. (English), and Cohen's close analysis of "The Story of the Four Captives," *PAAJR*, 29 (1960–61):55–131. For the shift to Christian Spain in the wake of the Almohade invasion, see *Sefer Ha-Qabbalah*, pp. 70ff. (English), 96ff. (Hebrew).

18. Habermann, *Sefer gezerot Ashkenaz ve-Zarefat*, p. 32 (my translation).

19. See, in general, Cohen's discussion of "The Symmetry of History" in his introduction to *Sefer Ha-Qabbalah*, pp. 189–222.

20. *Yosippon* was printed in Mantua, ca. 1480, Constantinople, 1510, Venice, 1544, Cracow, 1589. *Seder 'Olam Rabba*, *Seder 'Olam Zuta*, and *Sefer Ha-Qabbalah* were printed together in one volume along with *Megillat Ta'anit* and Ibn Daud's short *Zikhron Beney Romi* in Mantua, 1513, and in Venice, 1545. *Iggeret R. Sherira*, together with a Hebrew version of Josephus' *Contra Apionem*, were appended to the sixteenth-century chronicler Abraham Zacuto's *Sefer Yuḥasin*, printed in Constantinople, 1566, and in Cracow, 1580–81.

21. See M. Gaster, "The Scroll of the Hasmoneans," in his *Studies and Texts* (1928; reprinted New York, 1971), 1:165–83 (with bibliography and an English translation; for the Aramaic text, see 3:33–43). A new edition of the text accompanied by a linguistic study and a bibliography since Gaster is given by M. Z. Kedari, "Megillat Antiochus ha-'Aramit," *Bar-Ilan*, 1 (1963):81–105; 2 (1964):178–214.

22. Though by no means exceptional, the continual retrospective attribution of national calamity to the 9th of Ab remains a striking example of such thinking. The date is not biblically based. In II Kings 25:8–9, the First Temple is burned on the *seventh* day of the fifth month, while in Jer. 52:12, the *tenth* day is given. Concerning the destruction of both the First and Second Temples, Josephus (*The Jewish War*, 6:iv:5) and TB *Ta'anit* 29a refer to the 10th of Ab (the month "Lous" in Josephus). Nonetheless, the 9th of Ab became the accepted date for these as well as other catastrophes. Indeed, in Mishnah *Ta'anit* 4:4 we read: "Five misfortunes befell our fathers on the seventeenth of Tammuz and five on the ninth of Ab . . . On the ninth of Ab it was decreed that our fathers should

not enter the [Promised] Land, the Temple was destroyed the first and second time, Bethar was captured, and the city [Jerusalem] was ploughed up." Under the weight of such traditions it is not surprising to find the same tendency in later ages. Thus, the Expulsion from Spain in 1492 was placed on the 9th of Ab as well (Isaac Abravanel appears to have been the first to do so; see his commentary on Jer. 2:24), even though the last Jew seems to have left Spain by July 31, which was the 7th of Ab. See Y. Baer, *A History of the Jews in Christian Spain* (Philadelphia, 1961), 2:439.

23. They are discussed in detail by E. Mahler, *Handbuch der jüdischen Chronologie* (Leipzig, 1916), pp. 137–59. Though known to the Talmud (*Abodah Zarah* 9b), the Era of Creation was not to come into general use until Geonic times, at the earliest. All three eras are used side by side by Maimonides in *Mishneh Torah*, Shemitah ve-yobel, 10:4.

24. The Seleucid Era was thought by Isaac Israeli at the beginning of the fourteenth century to have begun with the alleged visit of Alexander the Great to Jerusalem. See his *Sefer yesod 'olam* (Berlin, 1777), p. 84. Maimonides equated *minyan shetarot* with "Malkhut Aleksandrus Muqdon" [The reign of Alexander of Macedon] in *Mishneh Torah*, Gerushin, 1:27. Cf. Mahler, *Handbuch*, pp. 144–46.

25. This was done by Rabbi David Ibn Abi Zimra, chief rabbi of Egypt, around 1511. See Hayyim Yosef David Azulai, *Shem ha-gedolim* (Livorno, 1774), fol. 17a. The use of the Seleucid Era had already declined long before in Europe. On the other hand, it continued to be used by the Jews of Yemen well into the twentieth century.

26. The issue surfaces sharply in G. Scholem's essay on "Tradition and Creation in the Ritual of the Kabbalists" in *On the Kabbalah and Its Symbolism* (New York, 1965), pp. 118–57). In the course of his discussion Scholem draws a stark contrast between kabbalistic ritual, which, rooted in myth and magic, actually effects changes in the upper worlds, and the commemorative rituals of Rabbinic Judaism which do not claim this power (unless themselves infused with new kabbalistic meaning). "Thus," he writes, "this history-saturated ritual was accompanied by no magical action. The rites of remembrance produce no *effect* . . . and what they 'conjure up' without the slightest gesture of conjuration is the memory, the community of generations, and the identification of the pious with the experience of the founding generation which received the Revelation. The ritual of Rabbinical Judaism makes nothing happen and *transforms* nothing. Though not devoid of feeling . . . there is something strangely sober and dry about the rites of remembrance with which the Jew calls to mind his unique historical identity" (*ibid.*, p. 121).

Upon reading this characterization one wonders, paradoxically, whether Rabbinic halakhah, ritual, and liturgy are not today in a position analogous to that of Jewish mysticism and kabbalah before Scholem unveiled their inner life through his epoch-making labors. Happily, with his customary candor Scholem himself recognizes the problem that his own description has raised. "The astonishing part of it," he continues, "is that a ritual which so consciously and emphatically rejected all cosmic implications should have asserted itself for so many generations with undiminished force, and even continued to develop. A penetrating phenomenology of Rabbinical Judaism would be needed to determine the nature of the powers of remembrance that made this possible and to decide whether other secret factors may not after all have contributed to this vitality." Such a phenomenology, alas, is not yet on the horizon.

27. The author of this lament (*'Esh tuqad be-qirbi*) is not known. The poem appears in many liturgies. See I. Davidson, *Ozar ha-shirah veha-piyyut* [Thesaurus of Medieval Hebrew Poetry] (New York, 1924), vol. 1, no. 7726. I have used *Seder tefillah le-ta'anit* [Fast-day prayers, Sephardic rite] (Amsterdam, 1726), fols. 83ff.

28. This particular force of *Ha lahma* is, I think, implicit within it. But it is also revealed indirectly, and somewhat ironically, by a variant that is found in certain Haggadah texts, where the reading becomes *ke-ha lahma*—"*like* this bread," or even *ha ke-lahma*—"this [is] *like* the bread." (See M. M. Kasher, *Haggadah shelemah* [3rd ed.; Jerusalem, 1967], in the critical apparatus to the text, p. 5.) The addition of the particle *ke* ("like") was apparently the work of a pedestrian mentality that could not tolerate the thorough equation implied in the original reading. Those who made the change not only created an outrageously ungrammatical Aramaic sentence; they simply missed the point. The alteration was flatly rejected in the sixteenth century by Rabbi Judah Loewe (MaHaRaL) of Prague, citing Exod. 17:32—"*that they may see the bread* wherewith I fed you in the wilderness, when I brought you forth from the land of Egypt" (*Geburot Ha-Shem* [New York, 1969], p. 218).

29. Mishnah *Pesahim* 10:5.

30. See M. Steinschneider, *Die Geschichtsliteratur der Juden* (Berlin, 1905), *passim*, and the texts published in such anthologies as Habermann, *Sefer gezerot Ashkenaz ve-Zarefat*, and S. Bernfeld, *Sefer ha-dema'ot* [The book of tears], 3 vols. (Berlin, 1924–26). A full corpus of medieval *selihot* and *qinot* ("laments") based on historial events remains a desideratum.

31. Edited with a German translation by S. Salfeld, *Das Martyrologium des Nürnberger Memorbuches* (Quellen zur Geschichte der Juden in Deutschland, vol. 3 [Berlin, 1898]). In the Introduction, pp. xvi-xxxix, there is a list of *Memorbücher* from fifty-five communities. Additional references in Steinschneider, *Geschichtsliteratur*, no. 24.

32. See M. Steinschneider, "Purim und Parodie," *MGWJ*, 47 (1903): 283–86. Another list, not complete, is given in *Encyclopedia Judaica* (English), vol. 13, s. v. "Purim." Second Purims were created well into

modern times. See C. Roth, "Some Revolutionary Purims (1790–1801)," *HUCA*, 10 (1935):451–83 (mostly on deliverances during the turmoil of the Napoleonic invasions of Italy).

33. See the poem *'Eluhu 'on* in *Divan Shemuel Ha-Nagid*, ed. D. Yarden (Jerusalem, 1966), pp. 4–14.

34. See the short account by Meir ben Isaac in Neubauer, *MJC*, 2:251; D. Kaufmann, "Le Pourim de Narbonne," *REJ*, 32 (1896):129–30.

35. The Hebrew text was published by M. Slatki, *Ner Mosheh* (Jerusalem, 1882) fols. 83–84. For the confusion of Syracuse as "Saragossa," see D. Simonsen, "Le Pourim de Saragosse est un Pourim de Syracuse," *REJ*, 59 (1910):90–95.

36. For the events, see the account of Samuel ben Saadya Ibn Danan in *Siddur 'ahabat ha-qadmonim* [Prayerbook according to the rite of Fez] (Jerusalem, 1889), fols. 12b–13a. A Spanish translation of the scroll read annually in memory of this occasion is given by F. Cantera Burgos, "El 'Purim' del Rey Don Sebastián," *Sefarad*, 6 (1945):224ff., and another in French by A. I. Laredo in his study of "Les Purim de Tanger," *Hespéris*, 35 (1948):193–203 (see 197–99, with facsimile). Cf. also G. Vajda, *Un recueil de textes historiques Judeo-Marocains* (reprinted from *Hespéris*, 25–26 [Paris, 1951]), pp. 15–17, with a French translation from a manuscript of Ibn Danan's account that contains some variations. The so-called "Purim de las bombas," sometimes confused with that of Sebastian, is entirely distinct and has a scroll of its own, relating the deliverance from the bombardment of Tangier by a French squadron in 1844 (see Laredo, pp. 199ff.).

37. Edited with English translation by G. Margoliouth, "Megillat Miṣṣraim, or the Scroll of the Egyptian Purim," *JQR* (o.s.), 8 (1896): 274–88. Several recensions of the scroll are extant. For an earlier "Egyptian Scroll" that refers to deliverance from the persecution of the Caliph Al-Hakim in 1012, see Jacob Mann, *The Jews in Egypt and in Palestine under the Fatimid Caliphs*, vol. 2 (Oxford, 1922; one vol. reprint, New York, 1970), appendix A, no. 8, pp. 31–38 (giving two versions).

38. For a list of such annual commemorative fasts, see L. Zunz, *Die Ritus des synagogalen Gottesdienstes* (Berlin, 1859), pp. 127–30, and the additions of D. Simonsen, "Freud und Leid: Locale Fest-und Fasttage im Anschluss an Zunzens Fastenabelle," *MGWJ*, 38 (1894):524–27.

39. On the events and their aftermath, see S. Spiegel, "Mi-pitgamey ha-'Akedah: Serufey Blois ve-hithadshut 'alilot ha-dam" [The martyrs of Blois and the renewal of ritual murder accusations], *Mordecai M. Kaplan Jubilee Volume* (New York, 1953), Hebrew section, pp. 267–87; R. Chazan, "The Blois Incident of 1171: A Study in Jewish Intercommunal Organization," *PAAJR*, 36 (1968):13–31.

40. Habermann, *Sefer gezerot Ashkenaz ve-Zarefat*, p. 126.

41. J. Katz, "Beyn TaTNU le-TaH ve-TaT" [Between 1096 and

1648–49], *Sefer ha-yobel le-Yitzhak Baer* (Jerusalem, 1961), pp. 318–37.

42. Shabbetai Katz, *Megillat 'Efah*, printed as an appendix to M. Wiener's edition of Solomon Ibn Verga's *Shebet Yehudah* (Hannover, 1856; reprint, 1924), p. 139.

43. *Pinqas Va'ad Arba Arazot* (Acta Congressus Generalis Judaeorum Regni Poloniae, 1580–1764), ed. I. Halperin (Jerusalem, 1945), no. 207, pp. 77–78.

44. From the printer's preface to *Selihot le-yom ha-'esrim le-Sivan*, n.p., n.d. [Cracow, 1650]. The entire preface was reprinted, along with the extant poems of Heller, by A. M. Habermann, "Piyyutav ve-shirav shel Rabbi Yom Tob Lipmann Heller," in *Li-kebod Yom Tob*, ed. J. L. Hacohen Maimon (Jerusalem, 1956), pp. 125ff. It is significant that Heller had earlier composed special *selihot* for a fast-day of the 14th of Heshvan in Prague emanating from the troubles of 1618–21, when the populace revolted and elected a new king. The printer now asked him why he would not write new *selihot* for the Cossack massacres as well. Heller replied that the two events are to be differentiated. The danger in Prague emanated from a general state of war in which the "destroyer does not distinguish between the righteous and the wicked" (citing TB *Baba Kama* 60a). The Cossack massacres were due to the same hatred of Jews as in all the calamities through the ages, and so the old *selihot* would suffice.

45. N. Wahrmann, *Meqorot le-toledot gezerot TaH ve-TaT: Tefillot u-selihot le-Kaf Sivan* [Sources for the history of the persecutions of 1648–49: prayers and selihot for the 20th of Sivan] (Jerusalem, 1949), p. 9.

46. Along with the Crusade chronicles they somehow came into the hands of Joseph Ha-Kohen in the sixteenth century (he quotes from them in his *Dibrey ha-Yamim* [Sabbionetta, 1554], fols. 57b–59a). None of the other sixteenth-century Jewish historians allude directly to what occurred at Blois. Although himself an Ashkenazic Jew, David Gans does not mention it, but states only that "in the year 4,931 the Jews encountered many troubles, and by divine grace they were saved" (*Zemah David* [Prague, 1591], fol. 55b).

3. IN THE WAKE OF THE SPANISH EXPULSION

1. First edition, Adrianople, 1554; second edition under the false imprint "Adrianople" (actually Sabbionetta, 1566–67). Frequently reprinted thereafter and translated, by the early nineteenth century, into

Yiddish, Latin, Spanish, and Ladino. The standard edition is now that of A. Shohat, with an introduction by Y. Baer (Jerusalem, 1947). German translation by M. Wiener, *Das Buch Schevet Jehuda* (Hannover, 1856; reprinted 1924). Spanish translation by F. Cantera Burgos, *Chevet Yehuda* (Granada, 1927). The fundamental studies are by F. (Y.) Baer, *Untersuchungen über Quellen und Komposition des Schebet Jehuda* (Berlin, 1923), and his "He'arot ḥadashot 'al Sefer Shebet Yehudah" [New notes on *Shebet Yehudah*], *Tarbiz*, 6 (1934–35):152–79. See also A. A. Neuman, "The *Shebet Yehudah* and Sixteenth-Century Jewish Historiography," *Louis Ginzberg Jubilee Volume* (New York, 1945), English section, pp. 253–73, reprinted in his *Landmarks and Goals* (Philadelphia, 1953), pp. 82–104; Y. H. Yerushalmi, *The Lisbon Massacre of 1506 and the Royal Image in the 'Shebet Yehudah'*, HUCA Supplement no. 1 (Cincinnati, 1976).

2. First edition, Constantinople, 1566; second edition, Cracow, 1580–81. The modern edition, full of gross errors, is by H. Filipowski, *Sefer Yuḥasin Ha-Shalem: Liber Juchassin sive Lexicon Biographicum et Historicum* (London-Edinburgh, 1857, reprinted with introduction and notes by A. H. Freimann, Frankfurt a.M., 1924). The need for a critical edition has been demonstrated vividly by J. L. Lacave, "Las fuentes cristianas del Sefer Yuḥasin," *Proceedings of the Fifth World Congress of Jewish Studies* (Jerusalem, 1972), 2:92–98. On Zacuto and his work, see F. Cantera Burgos, *El judío Salmantino Abraham Zacut* (Madrid, 1931), and *Abraham Zacut* (Madrid, 1935); A. A. Neuman, "Abraham Zacuto, Historiographer," *Harry Austryn Wolfson Jubilee Volume* (Jerusalem, 1965) 2:597–629; C. Roth, "The Last Years of Abraham Zacut," *Sefarad* 9 (1949):445–54; A. Shohat, "R. Abraham Zacut bi-yeshibat R. Yizhak Sholal bi-Yerushalayim" [Zacuto in the academy of R. Isaac Sholal in Jerusalem], *Zion*, 13–14 (1948–49):43–46; and the important recent study by M. Bet-Aryé and M. Idel, "Ma'amar 'al Ha-Qeẓ veha-'Iztagninut me-'et R. Abraham Zacut" [A treatise on the time of the redemption and on astrology by R. Abraham Zacut], *Kirjath Sefer*, 54 (1979):174–92.

3. Neither work was printed during Capsali's lifetime; both are now available in a critical edition by A. Shmuelevitz, S. Simonsohn and M. Benayahu, *Seder 'Eliyahu Zuta*, 2 vols. (Jerusalem, 1976–77). The Venetian chronicle occupies pages 215–327 of volume 2. A third volume of introductions and notes is expected. On Capsali, see H. H. Ben-Sasson, "Qavim li-temunat 'olamo ha-ruhani veha-ḥebrati shel kroniston Yehudi be-shilhey yemey ha-benayim" [Aspects of the spiritual and social world of a Jewish chronicler at the end of the Middle Ages], *Sefer Zikkaron le-Gedalyahu Alon* [G. Alon Memorial Volume] (Tel Aviv, 1970), pp. 276–91; S. Simonsohn, "Yehudey 'Eyropah ha-noẓrit ba-'aspaqlariah shel Seder 'Eliyahu Zuta" [The Jews of Christian Europe in the mirror of the

Seder 'Eliyahu Zuta], *Sefer Zikkaron le-Aryeh Leone Carpi: Scritti in memoria di Leone Carpi* (Jerusalem, 1963), pp. 64–71.

4. First edition, Ferrara, 1553. The Portuguese text was reprinted by J. Mendes dos Remédios, 3 vols. (Coimbra, 1906–8). English translation and study of the third part only by G. I. Gelbart, *A Consolation for the Tribulations of Israel: Third Dialogue* (New York, 1964). Complete English translation with introduction and notes by M. Cohen, *Samuel Usque's Consolation for the Tribulations of Israel* (Philadelphia, 1965). See also A. A. Neuman, "Samuel Usque: Marrano Historian of the Sixteenth Century," in *To Dr. R.: Essays . . . in Honor of the Seventieth Birthday of Dr. A. S. W. Rosenbach* (Philadelphia, 1946), pp. 180–203; reprinted in *Landmarks and Goals*, pp. 105–29.

5. First edition, Sabbionetta, 1554. Part III of this work, never published before, was edited by D. A. Gross, *Sefer dibrey ha-yamin . . . Heleq shelishi* (Jerusalem, 1955). H. H. Ben-Sasson has shown that, inexplicably, Gross omitted entire passages from the British Museum manuscript (see "The Reformation in Contemporary Jewish Eyes," *Proceedings of the Israel Academy of Sciences and Humanities*, 4 (1970):44, n.127). The English translation of Parts I–II by C. H. F. Bialloblotzky (*The Chronicles of Rabbi Joseph ben Joshua ben Meir the Sephardi*, 2 vols. [London, 1835–36]) is, unfortunately, of little value. The basic study is still I. Loeb, "Joseph Haccohen et les chroniqueurs juifs," *REJ*, 16 (1888):28–56, 212–35; 17 (1888):74–95, 247–71, and also as a separate offprint, Paris, 1888.

6. First published by M. Letteris with notes by S. D. Luzzatto (Vienna, 1852); reprinted Cracow, 1895. German translation by M. Wiener, *Emek habacha* (Leipzig, 1858). French translation by Julien Sée, *La vallée des pleurs* (Paris, 1881; reprinted with an introduction by J. P. Osier, Paris, 1981). Spanish translation by Pilar León Tello, *Emeq Ha-Bakha de Yosef Ha-Kohen* (Madrid–Barcelona, 1964). English translation (to be used with caution) by H. S. May, *The Vale of Tears* (The Hague, 1971).

7. First edition, Venice, 1587; second edition, Cracow, 1596. For later editions see Steinschneider, *Geschichtsliteratur*, no. 131. On the work itself, see A. David, *Mif'alo ha-historiografi shel Gedaliah Ibn Yahia ba'al Shalshelet ha-Qabbalah* [The historiographical work of Gedaliah Ibn Yahia], Hebrew University dissertation, Jerusalem, 1976.

8. First edition, Mantua, 1574–75; second edition, Berlin, 1794. Ed. D. Cassel, Vilna, 1864–66 (reprint, 3 vols., Jerusalem, 1970). On Azariah, see S. W. Baron "Azariah de' Rossi's Attitude to Life," *Israel Abrahams Memorial Volume* (New York, 1927), pp. 12–53; *idem*, "La méthode historique d'Azaria de' Rossi," *REJ*, 86 (1929):43–78. Both essays, somewhat abridged, appear in English in his *History and Jewish*

Historians (Philadelphia, 1964), pp. 174–204 and 205–39, respectively.

9. First edition, Prague, 1592, and frequently thereafter (see Steinschneider, *Geschichtsliteratur*, no. 132). On Gans as historian see M. Breuer, "Qavim li-demuto shel R. David Gans" [David Gans: A typological study], *Bar-Ilan*, 11 (1973):97–118; B. Degani, "Ha-mibneh shel ha-historiah ha-'olamit u-ge'ulat Yisrael be-*Ẕemaḥ David* le-R. David Gans" [The structure of world history and the redemption of Israel in *Ẕemaḥ David*], *Zion*, 45 (1980):173–200. For a general profile see A. Neher, *David Gans* (Paris, 1974).

10. I have deliberately listed only full-scale Jewish historical works, for only these properly belong to that historiographical phenomenon of the sixteenth century which we are attempting to explore. The list can obviously be expanded if we include partial or incidental chronicles of contemporary events or historical accounts that were not intended as independent works but were incorporated within books written in other, non-historiographical genres. For the moment we may note that an updated "supplement" to Abraham Ibn Daud's *Sefer Ha-Qabbalah* was completed under the same title in Fez, 1510, by a Spanish refugee, Abraham b. Solomon Ardutiel (not "of Torrutiel"). It was published by Neubauer, *MJC*, 1:101–14, and by A. Harkavy as an appendix to the sixth volume of the Hebrew translation of Graetz's history of the Jews (*Dibrey yemey Yisrael*, 6 [Warsaw, 1898]). Harkavy's edition has been reproduced with a new historical and bibliographical introduction by A. David, *Shetey kroniqot 'ibriot mi-dor gerush Sefarad* (Jerusalem, 1979; includes also the historical section of *Qiẕẕur Zekher Ẕaddiq* by Joseph b. Zaddik of Arévalo from *MJC*, 1:85–100). There is also a Spanish translation by F. Cantera Burgos, *El Libro de la Cabalá de Abraham ben Salomon de Torrutiel, y un fragmento histórico de José Ibn Zaddic de Arévalo* (Salamanca, 1928).

Other short "chronicles" of the Spanish expulsion have been published by A. Marx, "The Expulsion from Spain: Two New Accounts," *JQR* (o.s.), 20 (1907–8):240–71, and recently by Y. Hacker, "Kroniqot ḥadashot 'al gerush ha-Yehudim mi-Sefarad, sibbotav ve-toz'otav" [New chronicles concerning the expulsion of the Jews from Spain, its causes and consequences], *Sefer Zikkaron le-Yitzhak Baer* [Y. Baer Memorial Volume=*Zion*] 44 (Jerusalem, 1979):202–28. Italy in the sixteenth century produced several chronicles of local persecutions and expulsions in the wake of the Counter-Reformation. See, e.g., the chronicle of personal and general Jewish troubles in the Papal States by Benjamin Nehemiah b. Elnatan, published by I. Sonne as *Mi-Pavlo ha-rebi'i 'ad Pius ha-ḥamishi* [from Paul IV to Pious V] (Jerusalem, 1954).

11. Rich materials from several genres are brought together in H. H.

Ben-Sasson, "Galut u-ge'ulah be-'eynav shel dor goley Sefarad" [Exile and redemption in the eyes of the generation of the Spanish exiles], *Sefer Yobel le-Yitzhak Baer*, pp. 216–27, and his "Dor goley Sefarad 'al 'azmo" [The generation of the Spanish exiles on its fate], *Zion*, 26 (1961): 23–64.

12. Gersonides (Levi b. Gershom [RaLBaG]), *Perush 'al ha-Torah*, on Lev. 26:38.

13. Abravanel, *Perush nebi'im aharonim*, on Is. 43:6.

14. Zacuto, *Yuhasin*, ed. Filipowski–Freimann, p. 223. That the Spanish expulsion was perceived as one of the truly pivotal events in history is exemplified by its appearance on sixteenth-century Jewish calendars along with the creation of the world, the exodus from Egypt, the destruction of the Temple, etc. The significance of this has been noted by Y. Hacker, "Kroniqot hadashot," p. 202, n.6, citing examples from calendars printed in Constantinople in 1548 and 1568. I have in my possession a Hebrew calendar printed on one sheet in Mantua for the year [5]317 (1557). In the upper right-hand corner (somewhat damaged with a slight loss of text) there is a list of events with the years that have elapsed, which includes the Exodus, the building and destruction of the First Temple, the "Empire of Media and Persia," the "Greek Empire," "1,874 since [the beginning of] the Era of Contracts (*minyan shetarot*) and the end of prophecy (*hatimat hazon*) . . . ," the "[rise] of the religion of the Christians," the destruction of the Second Temple, the redaction of the Jerusalem Talmud and of the Babylonian Talmud . . . , "65 since the exile from Spain, 57 [*sic*] since the exile from Portugal."

15. See Hans Baron, *The Crisis of the Early Italian Renaissance* (Princeton, 1955), especially chs. 1–3.

16. This view derives from Yitzhak Baer. See his introduction to *Shebet Yehudah*, ed. Shohat, pp. 11, 13–14, as well as his *Galut* (Eng. trans.; New York, 1947), pp. 77ff.

17. See M. Benayahu, "Maqor 'al megorashey Sefarad be-Portugal ve-zetam 'aharey gezerat RaSaV le-Saloniki" [A source concerning the Spanish exiles in Portugal and their emigration after the persecution of 1506 to Salonika], *Sefunot*, 11 (1971–78):233–65.

18. *Dibrey ha-yamim le-malkhey Zarefat u-malkey Bet Ottoman ha-Togar* (Sabbionetta ed.), Preface.

19. See A. Shmuelevitz's brief examination of "Capsali as a Source for Ottoman History, 1450–1523," *International Journal of Middle East Studies*, 9 (1978):339–44.

20. Both works are extant in at least four manuscripts: Paris (Alliance, H81A); Berlin (Heb. 160); New York (Columbia University, K82); Moscow (Günzberg, 212). All of these also contain his Hebrew version, entitled *Mazib gebulot 'amim*, of Joannes Boemus' historical-geographical

work *Omnium gentium mores, leges et ritus* (Augsburg, 1520). See the excerpts published by R. Weinberg, "Yosef b. Yehoshua ha-Kohen ve-sifro *Mazib gebulot 'amim*," *Sinai*, 72 (1973):333–64.

21. See A. Neubauer, "Ha-ḥeleq ha-aḥaron min ha-ma'amar ha-shishi shel Sefer Yuḥasin le-R. Abraham Zacut" [The last section of the sixth part of *Sefer Yuḥasin*], *Tehilah le-Mosheh* (M. Steinschneider Festschrift; Leipzig, 1896), Hebrew section, pp. 209–18; Jirina Sedinova, "Non-Jewish Sources in the Chronicle by David Gans," *Judaica Bohemiae*, 8 (1972):3–15, and her "Czech History as Reflected in the Historical Work by David Gans," *ibid*. pp. 74–83. Among sixteenth-century Jewish works incorporating nc͡n ˙. wish history we may also properly include the chronology of Turkish sultans and the account of the reign of Suleiman the Magnificent in *Extremos y grandezas de Constantiopla*, written in Ladino by the sixteenth-century Salonikan rabbi Moses Almosnino, of which a Spanish abridgement by Jacob Cansino was published in Madrid in 1638.

22. *'Emeq Ha-Bakka*, ed. Letteris, pp. 102ff.; *Sefer Dibrey ha-yamim*, Sabbionneta ed., Part I, fol. 113a. Cf. also the account of the martyred messianic enthusiast Solomon Molkho in the latter work (Part II, fols. 207a–19b), introduced by the significant phrase, "And a shoot came forth from Portugal [*va-yeẓe ḥoter mi-Portugal*], Solomon Molkho was his name . . . ."

23. See Y. H. Yerushalmi, "Messianic Impulses in Joseph Ha-Kohen," to be published in the proceedings of the Colloquium on Sixteenth-Century Jewish Thought held at Harvard University in 1979. I have suggested in that paper that there were powerful messianic stimuli to the whole of sixteenth-century Jewish historiography.

24. See C. Berlin, "A Sixteenth-Century Hebrew Chronicle of the Ottoman Empire: The *Seder Eliyahu Zuta* of Elijah Capsali and Its Message," *Studies in Jewish Bibliography, History and Literature in Honor of I. Edward Kiev* (New York, 1971), especially pp. 26ff.

25. In this special sense Karl Löwith's remarks on Vico's notion of providence can be applied with some justice to Ibn Verga as well: "In spite of its supernatural origin, providence as conceived by Vico works . . . in such a 'natural,' 'simple,' and 'easy' way that it almost coincides with the social laws of the historic development itself. It works directly and exclusively by secondary causes in the 'economy of civil things,' as it works, less transparently, in the physical order" (*Meaning in History* [Chicago, 1949], p. 123).

26. Y. H. Yerushalmi, *The Lisbon Massacre of 1506 and the Royal Image in the 'Shebet Yehudah'*, Part III, pp. 35–66.

27. *Yuḥasin*, author's introduction, p. 1.

28. See Gans' introduction to Part II of *Zemaḥ David* where, after a

general apologia for presenting the reader with an account of gentile history and for drawing his information from non-Jewish sources, he feels constrained to enumerate no less than ten useful purposes that the book serves. In the ninth of these he states: "Since we are among the nations, strangers and sojourners with them, when they relate or ask us about the days of yore and the empires of old, we put our hands to our mouths and do not know what to answer. And so we seem to them like cattle that cannot distinguish between their right and left, or as though we were all born but the day before yesterday . . . ."

29. In ed. Sabbionetta, 1554, Zerahiah's poem is printed on the title page.

30. *Yosippon*, ed. Hominer, p. 43. Compare, in the seventeenth century, Joseph Delmedigo's list of recommended readings to the Karaite Zerah ben Menahem, which I have used as one of the superscriptions to this chapter. The historical works, largely those we have discussed here, are endorsed merely "to distract yourself in an hour of depression" (*le-ta'anug ha-nefesh bi-she'at ha-izzabon*). For the text see S. Assaf, *Meqorot le-toledot ha-ḥinnukh be-Yisrael* (Tel Aviv, 1936), 1:101.

31. One example from the eighteenth century will suffice. In discussing which historical works may or may not be read on the Sabbath, R. Jacob Emden observes that ". . . the book *Shebet Yehudah* should be forbidden on the Sabbath, even though many miracles that happened to our forebears are mentioned in it, because of the things that sadden and pain the souls of the readers. But on weekdays it is right and proper for every Jewish person to look into it and know its contents, since he will gain from it a number of words of wisdom, above all in the recounting of the wonders of the Lord for our holy people, which has been persecuted since the day it came into being, yet the eyes of the Lord have been upon us and He has not abandoned us to be annihilated. . . . Therefore I say that every Israelite is obligated to become thoroughly versed in that fine book in order to remember God's graces with us in all the generations, for we have not yet done with the many persecutions . . . and along the way he will learn sweet and precious things, and will acquire understanding in the methods of [Jewish-Christian] polemics, and the refutations of those men of evil who lead Israel astray . . ." (*Sefer mor u-qeziah*, Part II [Altona, 1761], no. 307).

32. Emden, *ibid.* Cf. Joseph Karo, *Shulḥan 'Arukh*, 'Oraḥ ḥayyim, no. 307, p. 16, and the gloss of Moses Isserles, *ad loc.*

33. *Me'or 'Einayim*, ed. Cassel, 1:182. The phrase *mai de-havah havah* derives from the Talmud (*Yoma* 5b), where the question of the manner in which Aaron and his sons were dressed in their priestly garments is temporarily rejected as being of purely antiquarian interest ("what was—was").

34. *Me'or 'Einayim*, 1:189.

35. *Ibid.*, 2:275.

36. As a result, during the printing itself some pages were destroyed, some were exchanged for altered versions, and some additions were made, all in an attempt to forestall or mitigate further criticism. These complexities have been elucidated from the original pages in his collection by I. Mehlman "Sebib Sefer *Me'or 'Einayim* le-R. Azariah min Ha-'Adumim: Shetey mahadurot la-defus ha-rishon" [On R. Azariah de' Rossi's *Me'or 'Einayim*: Two editions of the first printing], *Zer li-geburot* (S. A. Shazar Jubilee Volume) (Jerusalem, 1973), pp. 638–57; reprinted in his *Genuzot sefarim* [Bibliographical essays] (Jerusalem, 1976), pp. 21–39.

37. See D. Kaufmann, "Contributions à l'histoire des luttes d'Azaria de' Rossi," *REJ*, 33 (1896):77–87; *idem*, "La défense de lire le Meor Enayim d'Azaria de Rossi," *REJ* 38 (1899):280–81; S.Z.H. Halberstamm, "Sheloshah ketabim 'al debar Sefer Me'or 'Einayim," *Tehilah le-Mosheb*, Hebrew section, pp. 1–8; D. Tamar, "La-herem 'al ha-sefer Me'or 'Einayim" [Concerning the ban on *Me'or 'Einayim*], *Kirjath Sefer*, 33 (1958):378–79.

38. See the attack of R. Judah Loew b. Bezalel (MaHaRaL) of Prague, *Be'er ha-golah* (New York, 1969), pp. 126–41, and the report of a ban issued by Joseph Karo from his deathbed in Safed, published by Kaufmann in his aforementioned article in *REJ*, vol. 33.

39. *Me'or 'Einayim*, 1:214–19.

40. A striking instance in the sixteenth century of the most extreme antagonism to any non-literal interpretation of aggadah, is provided by the Safed Mishnaic scholar Joseph Ashkenazi. See G. Scholem, "Yedi'ot hadashot 'al R. Yosef Ashkenazi, ha-Tanna mi-Zefat" [New information on R. Joseph Ashkenazi, the 'Tanna' of Safed], *Tarbiz*, 28 (1959):59–89, 201–33. Considering the antagonism of MaHaRaL to the *Me'or 'Einayim* above, n.37), his own complex understanding of aggadah is also of considerable relevance. See J. Elbaum, "R. Judah Loew of Prague and his Attitude to the Aggadah," *Scripta Hierosolymitana*, 22 (1971):28–47.

41. The various chronicles produced in the seventeenth and eighteenth centuries no longer represent an innovative, dynamic phenomenon. At best, they never transcend the bounds of sixteenth-century Jewish historiography, and some are even regressive in outlook or in quality. Whatever the informative value or intrinsic interest of any single work, the approach to Jewish history is thoroughly conservative, moving in well-worn grooves even when updating the chronological record. To grasp this fully would require a detailed analysis of each work. For the moment I want only to indicate briefly how I think the better-known works should be viewed.

Some of these are, literally or metaphorically, appendages to the historiography of the sixteenth century. David Tebele Schiff's so-called "Part III" to Gans' *Ẓemaḥ David* (published together as *Ẓemaḥ David he-ḥadash* [Frankfurt a.M., 1692]) merely adds another hundred years' chronology to what Gans had written. Similarly with the anonymous addition to Joseph Ha-Kohen's *Dibrey ha-yamim* (not to *'Emek ha-bakha*; see M. Shulwass, *Zion*, 10 [1944–45]:78–79). Imanuel Aboab's historical excursus at the end of his Spanish defense of the Oral Law (*Nomologia, o discursos legales* [Amsterdam, 1629]), or even Joseph Sambari's chronicle *Dibrey Yosef* (selections in *MJC*, 1:115–62), belong in style and outlook to the previous century. The chronicles of the Cossack massacres of 1648–49 in Poland (*Yeven meẓulah, Ẓa'ar bat rabbim, Ẓuq ha-'ittim, Tit ha-yeven*), bypass sixteenth-century historiography altogether and, standing squarely within the Ashkenazic martyrological tradition, have their spiritual roots in the mentality of the twelfth-century Crusade chronicles. David Conforte's *Qore ha-dorot*, completed after 1677 and published in Venice in 1746, or Yehiel Heilprin's *Seder ha-dorot* (Karlsruh, 1768), are fully within the genre of the "chain of tradition."

In Holland there were some stirrings of historical interest, but mostly of local or contemporary scope. (See the survey by L. and R. Fuks of "Joodse Geschiedschrijving in de Republiek in de 17e en 18e Eeuw," *Studia Rosenthaliana*, 6 [1972]:137ff., reprinted in English as "Jewish Historiography in the Netherlands in the 17th and 18th Centuries," *Salo Wittmayer Baron Jubilee Volume* [Jerusalem, 1974], 1:433–66). The most comprehensive work produced was Menahem Man Amilander's *Sheyris Yisroel* (Amsterdam, 1743) intended as a Yiddish continuation to *Yosippon*. However, the only really important parts are those concerning Dutch Jewry itself. For the rest, the author repeats the information he found in *Shebet Yehudah* and other sixteenth-century works, and relies heavily on Basnage (see lecture 4). Throughout the seventeenth and eighteenth centuries no new path was taken in historical writing, the critical spirit of an Ibn Verga or Azariah de' Rossi did not reappear, the interest in the history of other peoples was not broadened in any significant way. As late as 1793 an edition of Abraham Farissol's sixteenth-century geographical work *'Iggeret 'orḥot 'olam* was printed in Prague, and in 1810 yet another, together with *Seder 'Olam Rabba, Seder Olam Zuta*, and Ibn Daud's *Sefer Ha-Qabbalah*, the same combination we found in the sixteenth-century editions (see lecture 2, n.20).

42. See I. Tishby, *Torat ha-ra veha-qelippah be-qabbalat ha-'Ari* [The doctrine of evil and 'Qelippah' in Lurianic Kabbalism] (Jerusalem, 1942), and G. Scholem, *Major Trends in Jewish Mysticism* (New York, 1954), ch. 7, "Isaac Luria and His School". On the meaning, spread, and impact of Lurianic Kabbalah at the end of the sixteenth century, see

Scholem, *Sabbatai Sevi: The Mystical Messiah* (Princeton, 1973), ch. 1, "The Background of the Sabbatian Movement", pp. 1–102.

4. MODERN DILEMMAS

1. On Basnage's history see M. Yardeni, "New Concepts of Post-Commonwealth Jewish History in the Early Enlightenment: Bayle and Basnage," *European Studies Review*, 7 (1977):245–58 (expanded version of her Hebrew Lecture in *Proceedings of the Sixth World Congress of Jewish Studies* [Jerusalem, 1975], 2:179–84).

2. "Et j'ose dire, qu'il n'a point paru d'Historien chez les Juifs mêmes, qui ait rassemblé un si grand nombre de Faits qui regardent leur Nation; quoi qu'ils eussent plus d'intérêt que nous à le faire; Au contraire, il y a chez eux une grande rareté d'Historiens, et une affreuse sécheresse dans les Memoires de ceux qui ont écrit (*Histoire des Juifs* [The Hague, 1716], 1:19).

3. *Ibid.*, pp. 20–21.

4. *Ibid.*, p. 21. He mentions by name Gedaliah Ibn Yahya, David Gans, Solomon Ibn Verga, and Abraham Zacuto.

5. An abridged one-volume Dutch translation by Buscar Graevius had appeared under the title: *Kort Begryp van de Geschiedenisse der Joden, dienende tot een Vervolg van Josephus* (Amsterdam, 1719).

6. Weisel, *Dibrey Shalom ve-'Emet* (Berlin, 1782; unpaginated), ch. 5.

7. *Ha-Me'assef* (Koenigsberg, 1783–84), 1:7.

8. "Dabar 'el ha-qore mi-to'elet dibrey ha-ḥayyim ha-qadmonim veha-yedi'ot ha-meḥubarot lahem," *ibid.*, pp. 7–25.

9. Zunz's impact as "'father" of modern Jewish scholarship has been widely discussed. The most recent critical evaluation is by L. Wieseltier, "*Etwas über die jüdische Historik*: Leopold Zunz and the Inception of Modern Jewish Historiography," *History and Theory*, 20 (1981):135–49.

10. On the founding of the Verein, see S. Ucko, "Geistesgeschichtliche Grundlagen der Wissenschaft des Judenthums (Motive des Kulturvereins vom Jahre 1819)," *Zeitschrift für die Geschichte der Juden in Deutschland*, 5 (1935):1–34. See also M. Meyer, *The Origins of the Modern Jew* (Detroit, 1967), pp. 162ff. The quotations from Wolf's essay that follow are from the translation by L. Kochan, "On the Concept of a Science of Judaism (1822) by Immanuel Wolf," *Leo Baeck Institute Yearbook*, 2 (1957):194–204.

11. See M. Wiener, "The Ideology of the Founders of Jewish Scientific Research," *YIVO Annual of Jewish Social Science*, 5 (1950):184–96; *idem, Jüdische Religion im Zeitalter der Emanzipation* (Berlin, 1933), ch. 3 (also in Hebrew trans. [Jerusalem, 1974]); N. N. Glatzer, "The Beginnings of Modern Jewish Studies," in *Studies in Nineteenth-Century Jewish Intellectual History*, ed. A. Altmann (Cambridge, Mass., 1964), pp. 27–45.

12. Quoted by M. Meyer, *The Origins of the Modern Jew*, p. 167.

13. The most sweeping indictment of nineteenth-century Wissenschaft, essential for an understanding of his own work, has been that of Gershom Scholem. See his "Mi-tokh hirhurim 'al ḥokhmat Yisrael," first published in *Luaḥ Ha-'Areẓ* in 1945, reprinted in his *Debarim be-go* (Tel Aviv, 1975), pp. 385–403. It should be noted that Scholem's milder "The Science of Judaism—Then and Now" (printed in *The Messianic Idea in Judaism*, pp. 304–13), is not a translation of that essay, but of a lecture given in German at the Leo Baeck Institute in London in 1957.

14. There is an important and provocative discussion of the modern writer's hostility toward history and his use of the historian "to represent the extreme example of repressed sensibility in the novel and theatre," in H. V. White, "The Burden of History," *History and Theory*, 5 (1966): 111–34.

15. For an exception, largely ignored in his own lifetime, see S. W. Baron, "Levi Herzfeld the First Jewish Economic Historian," *Louis Ginzberg Jubilee Volume* (New York, 1945), English section, pp. 75–104; reprinted in his *History and Jewish Historians*, pp. 322–43.

16. Spinoza, *Theologico-Political Treatise*, trans. R. H. M. Elwes (New York, 1955), ch. 3, p. 55.

17. Cited by K. Löwith, *Meaning in History* (Chicago, 1949), p. 110.

18. Löwith, *Meaning in History*, pp. 194–95.

19. P. Browe, *Die Judenmission im Mittelalter und die Päpste* (Rome, 1942), p. 310.

20. Perhaps the most radical and repercussive single example of this has been Scholem's treatment of the Sabbatian and post-Sabbatian messianic movements of the seventeenth and eighteenth centuries. Already in his iconoclastic essay "Miẓvah ha-ba'ah ba-'aberah" (*Knesset*, 2 [1937]: 347–92; trans. by H. Halkin as "Redemption through Sin," in *The Messianic Idea in Judaism*, pp. 79–141), he had announced his intention to demonstrate that "Sabbatianism must be regarded not only as a single continuous development which retained its identity in the eyes of its adherents regardless of whether they themselves remained Jews or not, but also, paradoxical though it may seem, as a specifically *Jewish* phenomenon to the end." Scholem remained faithful to this approach through subsequent decades of work, which culminated in his magisterial *Shabbetai Ẓebi veha-tenu'ah ha-Shabbeta'it bi-yemey ḥayyav* [S. Z. and the Sabbatian

Movement during his lifetime], 2 vols. (Tel Aviv, 1957); English trans. by R. J. Z. Werblowski, *Sabbatai Ṣevi, the Mystical Messiah* (Princeton, 1973). Reiterating his fundamental position, he wrote in the Preface: "I do not hold to the opinion of those . . . who view the events of Jewish history from a fixed dogmatic standpoint and who know exactly whether some phenomenon or another is 'Jewish' or not. Nor am I a follower of that school which proceeds on the assumption that there is a well-defined and unvarying 'essence' of Judaism, especially not where the evaluation of historical events are concerned." The work immediately evoked a flurry of criticism, much of it so intemperate and personal as to obscure what was really at stake. For a judicious overview of the controversy and some of the substantive issues involved, see D. Biale, *Gershom Scholem: Kabbalah and Counter-History* (Cambridge, Mass., 1979), pp. 155, 172ff., 192ff., and *passim* (with full bibliography).

21. On the conflict with Graetz and the Breslau Seminary, see most recently N. H. Rosenbloom, *Tradition in an Age of Reform: The Religious Philosophy of Samson Raphael Hirsch* (Philadelphia, 1976), pp. 106ff.

22. See Luzzatto's letter of June 5, 1860, to S. Y. Rapoport in his collected correspondence, *'Iggerot SHaDaL*, 2 vols. in 9 parts (Przemysl and Cracow, 1882–94; reprint, Jerusalem, 1967), 2 (no. 646):1367.

23. See A. Altmann's illuminating analysis of "Franz Rosenzweig on History," in *Between East and West: Essays Dedicated to the Memory of Bela Horovitz*, ed. A. Altmann (London, 1958), pp. 194–214; reprinted in his *Studies in Religious Philosophy and Mysticism* (Ithaca, 1969), pp. 275–91.

24. See the elaborate discussions of both points in Franz Rosenzweig, *The Star of Redemption*, trans. W. W. Hallo (New York, 1970), Part III, Book 1 (on the Jews), Book 2 (on the peoples of the world). For a lucid understanding of Rosenzweig's position and its implications see A. A. Cohen, *The Natural and the Supernatural Jew* (New York, 1962), pp. 120–48. See also the interesting comparison by K. Löwith of "M. Heidegger and F. Rosenzweig, or Temporality and Eternity," *Philosophy and Phenomenological Research*, 3 (1942–43):53–77, reprinted as "M. Heidegger and Franz Rosenzweig: A Postscript to *Being and Time*," in Löwith, *Nature, History and Existentialism, and Other Essays in the Philosophy of History*, ed. A. Levison (Evanston, 1966), pp. 51–78.

25. E. Rosenstock-Huessy, *Out of Revolution* (New York, 1964), p. 696.

26. For other contrasts between memory and history, and somewhat different emphases, see M. Halbwachs, *La mémoire collective* (Paris, 1950), pp. 68–79. Halbwachs' statement (p. 68) that "en général l'histoire ne commence qu'au point où finit la tradition, moment où s'éteint ou se décompose la mémoire sociale," would not explain traditional Jew-

ish historiography of the types we have examined in the previous lectures, but is eminently applicable to modern Jewish historiography.

27. I am concerned here specifically with the meager influence of actual historical research and writing. Undoubtedly the "historicizing" of Jewish tradition since the early nineteenth century has been widespread, but only in the vague and general sense of viewing the tradition as historically conditioned and mutable rather than as revealed and eternal. That these changes were engendered by the work of Jewish historians is doubtful; that modern philosophies of Judaism have not come to grips with the cumulative results of historical scholarship is, I think, demonstrable. Appeals to history can be made without necessarily appealing to historians. It is this distinction that I find missing, for example, in N. Rotenstreich's otherwise suggestive book entitled *Tradition and Reality: The Impact of History on Modern Jewish Thought* (New York, 1972). Of the six figures considered, four were, of course, themselves historians (Zunz, Krochmal, Graetz, Dubnow). As for the other two, the Zionist theoretician Ahad Ha-Am and the great Hebrew poet Hayyim Nahman Bialik, I do not think that Rotenstreich himself would argue that a confrontation with historical scholarship was a decisive formative influence in the thought of either. A key issue is raised by Rotenstreich's statement (p. 77) that "the rise of historical consciousness in Jewish thought brought about a weakening of the bonds of tradition," a causality that seems to me the reverse of what had initially transpired.

28. The quotations that follow are from the English translation by Ben Halpern, *Partisan Review*, 23 (1956):171–87.

29. "Without forebears [*ohne Vorfahren*], without marriage, without heirs, with a fierce longing for forebears, marriage and heirs [*mit wilder Vorfahrens-, Ehe- und Nachkommenslust*]" (Franz Kafka, *Diaries* [New York, 1949], 2:207; *Tagebücher* [n.p. (Frankfurt), 1967], p. 40; entry for January 21, 1922). That "forebears" represented more than biological ancestry may be seen in the famous *Letter to His Father* (bilingual ed.; New York, 1966), pp. 75ff., where the father is accused of having handed down only the vulgar shards of his Judaism. For the reading of Graetz see the diary entry for November 1, 1911.

30. From the draft of an address at the opening of the Freies Jüdisches Lehrhaus in Frankfurt, printed in *Franz Rosenzweig: His Life and Thought*, ed. N. N. Glatzer (New York, 1961), p. 229.

31. The nineteenth-century view of Jewish history as predominantly a history of culture and suffering was ultimately a metamorphosis of the medieval Jewish preoccupation with martyrology and the "chain of tradition," and may well constitute the one line of continuity between Wissenschaft and the Middle Ages. The rejection of the "lachrymose conception of Jewish history" owes much to Salo Baron, who coined the

phrase early in his career, and has actively combatted this view throughout his work.

32. For specific examples see my "Clio and the Jews," pp. 609–11.

33. Though not conscious of it when I first wrote these lines, I have subsequently realized that Nietzsche had already pointed to insomnia as a metaphor for obsession with history when he declared: "Thus even a happy life is possible without remembrance, as the beast shows; but life in any true sense is absolutely impossible without forgetfulness. Or, to put my conclusion better, there is a degree of sleeplessness, of rumination, of 'historical sense,' that injures and finally destroys the living thing, be it a man or a people or a system of culture" (*The Use and Abuse of History*, trans. A. Collins [Indianapolis–New York, 1957], p. 7).

34. Jorge Louis Borges, "Funes el memorioso," in his *Ficciones* (Buenos Aires, 1956), pp. 123, 125. I have used the English translation by Anthony Kerrigan in his edition of *Ficciones* (New York, 1962), pp. 112, 114.

POSTSCRIPT

1. A. R. Luria, *The Man with a Shattered World*, tr. Lynn Solotaroff, foreword by Oliver Sacks (Cambridge, Mass., 1987); *idem*, *The Mind of a Mnemonist*, tr. Lynn Solotaroff, foreword by Jerome Bruner (Cambridge, Mass., 1987).

2. Luria, *The Mind of a Mnemonist*, p. 67.

3. "... wir alle an einem verzehrenden historischen Fieber leiden und mindestens erkennen sollten, das wir daran leiden." F. Nietzsche, "Vom Nutzen und Nachteil der Historie für das Leben" (= *Unzeitgemässe Betrachtungen*, II), in: *Werke in drei Banden* ed. Karl Schlechta. Bd. I (München, 1966), p. 210.

4. *Ibid.*, p. 213: "... es ist aber ganz und gar unmöglich, ohne Vergessen überhaupt zu *leben.*"

5. *Ibid.*, p. 214: "... davon, dass man ebenso gut zur rechten Zeit zu vergessen weiss, als man sich zur rechten Zeit erinnert; davon, dass man mit kräftigem Instinkte herausfühlt, wann es notig ist, historisch, wann, unhistorisch zu empfinden. Dies gerade ist der Satz, zu dessen Betrachtung der Leser eingeladen ist: *das Unhistorische und das Historische ist gleichermassen für die Gesundheit eines einzelnen, eines Volkes und einer Kultur nötig.*"

6. Freud, *Totem and Taboo*, *Civilization and Its Discontents*, and, above all, *Moses and Monotheism*. See now also the hitherto lost "metapsycholog-

ical" text of 1915 recently published as *Übertragungsneurosen: Ein bisher unbekanntes Manuskript*, ed. Ilse Grubrich-Simitis (Frankfurt, 1985); bilingual edition: *A Phylogenetic Fantasy,* tr. Axel Hoffer and Peter T. Hoffer (Cambridge, Mass., 1987). The critique of Lamarckism in general and of Freud's psycho-Lamarckism in particular has generated an abundant literature. For the essential points see Stephen Jay Gould, *Ontogeny and Phylogeny* (Cambridge, Mass., 1977), pp. 155–61 and *passim*; Frank J. Sulloway, *Freud, Biologist of the Mind* (New York, 1979), pp. 274f., 439ff.

7. Freud, too old and ill to attend, sent Anna to read only one short section from the as yet unpublished third part of *Der Mann Moses und die monotheistische Religion* (III.2.C: "Der Fortschritt in der Geistigkeit") which contains the passage quoted here. See *Internationale Zeitschrift für Psychoanalyse und Imago*, 24 (1939), pp. 6–9 and the program of the congress in the *Korrespondenzblatt* (*ibid.*, pp. 363f.).

8. *Le Monde,* May 2, 1987, p. 9.

Index

Aboab, Imanuel: *Nomologia,* 140n.41

Abraham, 13, 38

Abravanel, Isaac, 59

Aggadah, rabbinic, 16–17; anachronism in, 17, 18–20; historicity of, 18, 123n.19; and relations between Jews and gentiles, 36; subjected to historical scrutiny, 58, 71–72; literal interpretation of, 72, 139n.40

Akedah: as paradigm for martyrdom, 38–39

Akiba, Rabbi, 24

Alexander Jannaeus, 25

Alexandrian Jewry, 70

Almosnino, Moses, 137n.21

Amilander, Menahem Man, 82, 140n.41

Anachronism, historical: in rabbinic literature, 17, 18–20; rabbinic awareness of, 19, 123n.21

Anno mundi, 41

Apocalyptic literature, 36–37

Arabic culture, influence of, 33

Archetypes and archetypal thinking, 8–9, 36, 38, 122n.5

Ardutiel, Abraham b. Solomon, 135n.10

"Ashkenaz," 36

Ashkenazi, Joseph, 139n.40

Ashkenazic Jews, 38, 46, 51, 140n.41

Assimilation, creative, 85

Assyria, 21–22

Babylonia, 15, 22, 37, 41, 128n.17

Bar Kochba, 24

Baron, Salo Wittmayer, 81, 87, 132–33; *Social and Religious History of the Jews,* 95

Basnage, Jacques, 81–82, 140n.41

Benjamin Nehemiah b. Elnatan, 135n.10

Bible: command to remember in, 5, 9–10, 119n.1; archetypes in, 8; as history, 12–15, 121–24n.10; historical books of, 15; public readings of, 15–16, 41, 122n.14; and modern scholarship, 17

Blois martyrdom, 48–49, 51, 52

"Books of wars" *(sifrey milhamot),* 69

Borges, Jorge Luis, 102

Breslau seminary, 92

Browe, Peter, 90–91

Burckhardt, Jakob, 10

Calendars, Jewish, 40–41; *Megillat Ta'anit,* 20; subjected to historical scrutiny, 58; expulsion of Jews from Spain added to, 136n.14

Capsali, Elijah, 57, 58, 63, 65

"Chain of tradition" *(shalshelet haqabbalah),* 31, 66, 81, 126n.2, 144n.31; Maimonides on, 32, 126n.5; survival of, literature, 40

China, historiography of, 119nn.3, 4

Chmielnitzky, Bogdan, 49

Christendom: and meaning in history, 8; custom of reading historical chronicles, 34; archetype for, 36; struggle with Islam, 65;

unhistorical quality of, 90; and conversion of Jews, 90–91; Franz Rosenzweig on, 93

Chronicles, Jewish historical: biblical, 13–15; Hellenistic, 15; medieval, 34–36; of the Crusades, 37–39; of the seventeenth and eighteenth centuries, 139–40n.41

Chronology, Jewish systems of, 41

Cohen, Gerson, 39

Collective memory, 5, 15; in Middle Ages, 42–52; decay of, 86; modern historiography at odds with, 93–95, 143n.26

Columbia University, 81

Conforte, David, 140n.41

Conquista de México, La (Gómara/ Ha-Kohen), 63

Consolaçam as tribulaçoens de Israel (Usque), 57, 62

Conversion of Jews in Middle Ages, 90–91

Cossack massacres, 49–50, 51, 140n.1

Council of Four Lands, 50

Covenant: eternal, 10, 21; demands memory of both God and Israel, 119n.1

Crusades: Hebrew chronicles of, 37–39; compared with Cossack massacres, 49

Deuteronomic history, 9–10, 12

Dibrey ha-yamim le-malkhey Zaréjat u-malkhey Bet Ottoman ha-Togar (Ha-Kohen), 57, 61, 62, 64, 67

Dibrey Shalom ve-'Emet (Weisel), 82

Dubnow, Simeon, 87, 95

Eastern Europe, 49–51, 87

"Edom," as connotation for Christendom, 36

Egypt, 48

"Egyptian Purim," 48

Eliade, Mircea, 119n.2

Elijah, 47

Emden, Jacob, 138n.31

'Emeq ha-Bakha (Ha-Kohen), 57, 62, 64

Era, Seleucid *(minyan shetarot)*, 41, 129nn.24, 25

Era of Creation, 41, 129n.23

Eras, 41

"Esau," 36

Esther, book of, 47–48

Exodus from Egypt, 11, 12, 120n.5; contrasted with exile from Jerusalem, 43–44

Far Eastern civilizations, 7, 119n.3

Farissol, Abraham, 140n.41

Fast-days, post-biblical, 48–50, 51, 52, 132n.44

Feast days and festivals, as channel for memory, 11–12, 40. *See also* Holidays and holy days

First Temple, 39

France: "Zarefat" as, 36; persecutions in, 46; Purim of Narbonne, 47; Blois blood-libel, 48–49, 51, 52; Joseph Ha-Kohen on history of, 64–65

Gans, David, 58, 63, 66

Gans, Edouard, 86

Germany: "Ashkenaz" as, 36; persecutions in, 46; historiographic revolution in, 74; spread of Haskalah in, 82, 83; scholarship in, 88, 92

Gersonides, 59

Ginzberg, Louis, 18

Gnostic influence, 73

God: and biblical command to remember, 5, 119n.1; and dialectic of obedience and rebellion, 8; known only "historically," 9; acts of historical intervention by, 11; true hero of history, 12

Gog and Magog, 37, 65

Graetz, Heinrich, 87, 88, 92, 95, 98

Granada: victory of, and Second Purim, 46–47

Greek historiography, 7–8, 15, 119–20n.4

Ha-Derashah (Hazaz), 97, 99, 100–101

Hadrian, 25

Haggadah (Passover), 44, 45, 130n.28

Ha-Indiah ha-hadashah (Gómara/Ha-Kohen), 63

Ha lahma 'anya, variant readings, 44, 130n.28

Halakhah, rabbinic, 40, 52

Halbwachs, Maurice, xv, 143n.26

Halevi, Judah, 120n.6

Halevi, Zerahiah, 67

Haman, 36

Hanukkah, benediction, 25, 125–26n.38

Ha-sibbah ha-tib'it ("natural cause"), 65

Haskalah, 82, 83

Hasmonean dynasty, rabbinic attitudes to, 20, 24, 25, 125n.32

Hassidism, 97–98

Hazaz, Haim, 97, 99, 100–101

Hebrew literature, modern, 97

Heilprin, Yehiel, 32, 140n.41

Heine, Heinrich, 83

Hellenistic-Jewish literature, 58

Hellenistic period: Jewish historiography of, 15, 122n.13

Heller, Yom Tob Lipmann, 50, 51, 132n.44

Heraclitus, 10

Herodotus, 7–8

Herzfeld, Levi, 142n.15

Hirsch, Samson Raphael, 92

Histoire du peuple Juif (Basnage), 81–82

Historia general de las Indias (Gómara/Ha-Kohen), 63

Historians, modern Jewish: initial difficulties of, 87–88; and secularization of Jewish history, 91; and restoration of memory, 93–94; increasing specialization of, 95–96; choice of subject matter, 100, 102

Historical poetry, biblical, 43, 121–22n.10; *selihot* (penitential prayers), 45–46, 48, 49, 50, 51, 132n.44

Historical writing: low esteem for, in pre-modern Jewry, 65–69, 71, 73

Historicizing of Judaism, 91–92

Historiography: and collective memory of Jewish people, 5–6, 42–52; in India, 7, 25–26, 119n.3; Greek, 7–8, 15, 119–20n.4; Hellenistic-Jewish, 15, 122n.13; Islamic, 33, 65; Spanish, 37; Italian Renaissance, 60, 69, 92; French, 64–65, 88; German, 74, 88, 92; Chinese, 119nn.3, 4; Dutch Jewish, 140n.41

—biblical Jewish: treatment of time in, 13–14, 17–19; concreteness of, 13–14, 17; and historical books of Bible, 15; and prophecy, 15, 122n.11; lost works, 15, 122n.12; and modern scholarship, 17

—post-biblical Jewish: gap in, 16; Talmudic, 18, 123n.19; comparative lack of, in rabbinic literature, 20–26; prominence assigned to, in sixteenth century, 62, 64

—medieval Jewish: scarcity of, 31–34, 52; kinds of, 34–39; sche-

matic views of, 39; and Hebrew printing, 40; collective memory in Middle Ages, 42–52; new value assigned to, in sixteenth century, 62
—sixteenth-century Jewish: resurgence of writing, 57–64; awareness of novelty, 61–62; messianic themes in, 64–65; low esteem for, 65–69, 71, 73; "books of wars," 69; non-Jewish historical sources, 72
—seventeenth- and eighteenth-century Jewish, 73–75, 139–40n.41; of Cossack massacres, 140n.41
—modern Jewish (nineteenth and twentieth centuries): early efforts, 81–84; Wissenschaft, 84–89, 92, 100, 144n.31; origins of new spirit of, 85–86; and nationalism, 88–89; tension in, 89; secularization of, 89–91; historicizing of, 91–92; and collective memory, 93–95, 143n.26; as vocation, 93; lack of impact on Jewish people, 96, 144n.27; and anti-historical attitudes, 92–93, 96–97

Historisches Journal, 74
History: myth versus, 6–7, 10, 99, 119n.2; meaning in, 8, 10, 15, 119n.4; cyclical, 10, 42, 120–21n.7, 108n.14; resistance to novelty, 51; first chair of Jewish history, 81; political, social, economic, 88; providence in, 90, 137n.25; and "normative Judaism," 92; divorce from literature, 100; "terror of," 119n.2; "recurrence," 121n.7; "lachrymose conception" of, 144n.31. *See also* Collective memory; Historiography; Memory; Time

Holidays and holy days, 42–43. *See also* Feast days and festivals
Holland, 81, 82, 140n.41
Holocaust, 98

Ibn Abi Zimra, Rabbi David, 129n.25
Ibn Daud, Abraham, 37, 39, 40
Ibn Ezra, Moses, 33, 34
Ibn Nagrela, Samuel, 46
Ibn Verga, Joseph, 68
Ibn Verga, Solomon, 33–34, 58, 64, 137n.25; *Shebet Yehudah,* 33–34, 57, 60, 62, 65, 67–69, 128n.31
Ibn Yahia, Gedaliah, 57, 58, 60, 63, 66
Ibn Yahia, Tam, 35–36, 60, 67
'*Iggeret 'orḥot 'olam* (Farissol), 140n.41
Iggeret Rab Sherira Gaon, 32, 40
'*Iggeret Teman* (Maimonides), 32
India, historiography of, 7, 25–26, 119n.3
Isaac: binding of, 38
"Ishmael": as connotation for Islam, 36
Islam: and meaning in history, 8; archetype for, 36; struggle with Christendom, 65
Israel: and biblical command to remember, 5, 9–10, 119n.1; and meaning in history, 8, 10, 14; function of history in ancient, 14, 15
Italy: city-states in, 60; Renaissance humanism of, 60, 69, 92; ban on Azariah de' Rossi's book in, 71–73

Jerusalem, fall of, 22
Jewish Antiquities (Josephus Flavius), 16
Jewish Theological Seminary (Breslau), 92

Jewish War (Josephus Flavius), 16
Jose ben Halafta, 20
Joseph b. Zaddik of Arévalo, 135n.10
Joseph Ha-Kohen, 58, 60, 122n.15; translations by, 63; *Dibrey ha-yamim,* 57, 61, 62, 64–65, 67; *'Emeq ha-Bakha,* 57, 62, 64
Josephus Flavius, 16, 35, 61
Joshua ben Levi, Rabbi, 23
Judah Loewe b. Bezalel (MaHa-RaL) of Prague, 130n.28
Judenmission im Mittelalter und die Päpste, Die (Browe), 90–91

Kabbalah, 52, 72, 73–74
Kabbalistic ritual, 129n.26
Kafka, Franz, 98, 144n.29
Karo, Joseph, 139n.38
Katz, Rabbi Shabbetai, 50

Law, Jewish: and aggadah, 19; fulfillment of, 24. *See also* "Chain of tradition" (Oral Law)
Legends of the Jews, The (Ginzberg), 18
"Letter of Aristeas," 58
Lex talionis, 18
Literature, modern Hebrew, 97–98
Lithuania, 50
Liturgy. *See* Ritual
López de Gómara, Francisco, 63
Löwith, Karl, 90
Luria, Isaac, 73–74
Luzzatto, Samuel David, 92

Maccabees, battles of the, 25
MacLeish, Archibald, 18
Maimonides, 32, 33, 126–27n.5
Mainz, 38
Manasseh of Judah, 10–11, 15
Mantua, 58, 71
Marranos, Portuguese, 64

Martyrdom: under the Romans, 25, 125n.37; at Blois, 48–49, 51, 52; during Crusades, 37–39, 49
Masada, 99
Maskilim, 74
Me'assef, 83
Medieval Jewry: indifference to history of, 31–34, 52; and collective memory, 42–52. *See also* Historiography, medieval Jewish
Megillah ("scroll"), 47
Megillat Antiochus, 40
Megillat 'Efah, 50
Megillat Mizrayim, 48
Megillat Ta'anit, 20
Meinecke, Friedrich, 92
Memorbücher, 46
Memory: reciprocal demand of God and Israel, 5, 119n.1; *zakhor,* 5; biblical injunction, 5, 9–10, 11, 15; crucial to faith, 9; importance of *how* events happened, 11; importance of ritual and recital, 11–12, 15, 40; and search for a past, 99; conditions action, 99. *See also* Collective memory
Me'or 'Einayim (Azariah de' Rossi), 57–58, 60, 69–75; banned, 71–73; printing of, 74, 139n.36
Mesopotamia, 12
Messiah, coming of the, 23, 24, 36–37
Messianism, 24–25, 39, 64–65, 74, 101, 137nn.22, 23
Metahistorical myth, 73–74, 98
Midrash, 16, 21, 45
Miller professorship, 81
Minyan shetarot (Seleucid Era), 41, 139nn.24, 25
Miracles, 25
Molkho, Solomon, 137n.22

Mordecai, 36
Moriah, Mount, 38
Mosconi, Judah, 35
Moses, 9, 13, 19
Myth: preferred to history, 6–7, 10, 73–74, 99, 119n.2; Near Eastern motifs in aggadah, 16; metahistorical, 73–74, 98. *See also* Archetypes and archetypal thinking

Narbonne, Purim of, 47
Nationalism, 88–89
"Natural cause" *(ha-sibbah ha-tib'it),* 65
Near Eastern mythological motifs, 16
Nebuchadnezzar, 22
Netherlands, The. *See* Holland
Niebuhr, Barthold, 74
Nietzsche, Friedrich Wilhelm, 145n.33
Ninth of Ab *(Tish'ah be-'Ab),* 40–41, 43, 44, 128–29n.22
"Normative Judaism," 92
Nuremberg, 46

On the Concept of a Science of Judaism (Wolf), 83, 84
Oral Law. *See* "Chain of tradition"
Ottoman Empire, 47, 57, 63, 64–65. *See also* Islam

Padua, 57
Passover, 44, 45, 130n.28
Pentateuchal commentary, 59
Pentateuchal narratives, 15
Pharisees, 25
Philo of Alexandria, 58
Philosophy, Jewish, 72, 85–86
Poetry, historical, 43, 121–22n.10; *selihot* (penitential prayers), 45–46, 48, 49, 50, 51, 132n.44
Poetry, oral, 11

Poland, 49–50, 51, 140n.41
Portuguese Jewry, 47; exiles, 35; forced conversion, 59; expulsion, 60
Portuguese Marranos, 64
Prague, 58, 71
Printing, Hebrew: and the medieval historical legacy, 40
Prophets: and injunction to remember, 9–10; and meaning in history, 15, 122n.11; the Rabbis as successors to, 21, 24, 124n.28
Proust, Marcel, 5
Providence in history, 90, 137n.25
Purim, 40; "Egyptian," 48
"Purim de las bombas," 131n.36
Purim of Narbonne, 47
"Purim of Saragossa," 47
"Purim Sebastiano," 47
Purims, Second, 46–48, 131n.36

Qore ha-dorot (Conforte), 140n.41

Rabbinical council at Yabneh, 15, 16
Rabbinic law: and *lex talionis,* 18; transmission of, 31
Rabbinic literature, classical, 16–17; treatment of time in, 17–18; and historiography, 18; and post-biblical events, 20–26. *See also* Aggadah, rabbinic; Midrash; Talmud
Rabbinic ritual, 42–43, 129n.26
Rabbinic scholars, history of, 57
Rabbis, Talmudic: lack of historiography among, 20–26; as successors to the prophets, 21, 24, 124n.28; attitudes toward messianic activism, 24–25
Ranke, Leopold von, 74–75
"Recurrence," 121n.7

Index

153

Redemption: linked to destruction, 23–24; and Passover Seder, 44; imminence of, 64
Renaissance humanistic historical writing, 60, 69, 92
Resnais, Alain, 5
Rhineland, mass suicide in (Ashkenazic communities), 38
Ritual: preferred to history, 6–7, 51, 119n.2; memory flowing through, 11, 15, 40; rabbinic, 42–43, 129n.26; Passover, 44; kabbalistic, 129n.26. See also Collective memory
Ritual murder, 49
Roman Empire, 22, 23; uprisings against, 24, 39; martyrdom of scholars, 25, 125n.37
Rosenstock-Huessy, Eugen, 93
Rosenzweig, Franz, 92, 98
Rosh Ha-shanah, 42
Rossi, Azariah de', 58, 60, 64; Me'or 'Einayim, 57, 69–75, 139n.36
Rotenstreich, N., 144n.27
Roth, Philip, 99

Sabbatianism, 142–43n.20
Safed (Palestine), 71
Sambari, Joseph, 140n.41
Samuel bar Nahmani, Rabbi, 24–25
Samuel ben Nahman, Rabbi, 22
"Saragossa, Purim of," 47
Schiff, David Tebele, 140n.41
Scholarship, modern Jewish historical orientation of, 86–87. See also Historiography, modern Jewish
Scholem, Gershom, 74, 87, 129–30n.26, 142nn.13, 20
Scriptures, public reading of, 15–16, 41, 122n.14
Scroll. See Megillah
Scroll of Esther, 47

Sebastian, Dom, 47
Second Purims, 46–48, 131n.36
Second Temple period, 39; history of (Yosippon), 34–35
Secularization of Jewish history, 89–91
Secularization of the Jewish people, 83
Seder 'Eliyahu Zuta (Capsali), 57, 63, 65
Seder ha-dorot (Heilprin), 32, 140n.41
Seder 'Olam Rabba, 20, 40, 124n.26
Seder 'Olam Zuta, 40
Seder Tanna'im va-'Amora'im, 31–32
"Sefarad," 36
Sefer Fernando Cortes (Gómara/Ha-Kohen), 63
Sefer Ha-Qabbalah (Ibn Daud), 37, 39, 40
Sefer Yuhasin (Zacuto), 57, 60, 63
Seleucid Era (minyan shetarot), 41, 129nn.24, 25
Seleucus Nicator, 41
Selihot (penitential prayers), 45–46, 48, 49, 50, 51, 132n.44
Sephardic Jews, 58
Shaitan, Ahmed, 48
"Shalshelet ha-qabbalah." See "Chain of tradition"
Shalshelet ha-Qabbalah (Ibn Yahia), 57, 63
Shebet Yehudah (S. Ibn Verga), 33–34, 57, 60, 62, 65, 138n.31; "natural cause," 65; popularity of, 67–69
Shelomoh bar Shimshon, 38
Sherira, 32
Sheyris Yisroel (Amilander), 82, 140n.41
Sicily, 47
Sifrey milhamot ("books of wars"), 69

Sin, nature of: in destruction of First and Second Temples, 22

Sippurey Veneziah (Capsali), 57, 63

Social and Religious History of the Jews (Baron), 95

Spain: Golden Age of Spanish Jewry, 33; as "Sefarad," 36; historiography of, 37; and messianic interpretation of history, 39; and Second Purim for Granadan victory, 46; Hispano-Jewish aristocracy, 65; Jewish culture in, 85

Spain, expulsion from: exiles, 35, 58; historical writing on, 57, 59–65, 68, 135n.10; significance of, 59–60, 136n.14; date of, 129n.22

Spinoza, 89

Star of Redemption (Rosenzweig), 92

Suleiman the Magnificent, 48

Talmud, 16–25 *passim;* quotations from aggadah, 19, 23; little interest in recording current events, 21; and Jews of Middle Ages, 45; and massacre of Alexandrian Jewry, 70

Talmudic period, history of, 18, 21, 32–33, 123n.19

Tam, Rabbi Jacob (Rabbenu Tam), 49, 52

Temple, destruction of: reasons for, 22, 23, 125n.29; fast-days linked to, 40–41; era of, 41

Thibaut, Count, 48

Time: mythic and ritual abolition of, 6–7, 119n.2; linear vs. cyclical, 10, 42, 120–21n.7; in biblical historiography, 13–14, 17; in rabbinic literature, 17; Hebrew and Greek perceptions of, 119–20n.4. *See also* Archetypes;

Collective memory; Memory; Myth

Tish'ah be-'Ab. See Ninth of Ab

Tit ha-yeven, 140n.41

Torah she-be'al peh ("oral" law), 19

Torah she-biketab (written law), 19

Trompf, G. W., 120–21n.7

Turkey, 48. *See also* Ottoman Empire

Ukraine, 49

Usque, Samuel, 57, 58, 62, 64

Venice, 57

Verein für Cultur und Wissenschaft der Juden, 84, 86

Vico, Giovanni Battista, 137n.25

Voltaire, 89

Weisel, Naftali Zvi, 82

Wissenschaft des Judentums, 84, 86, 87, 88, 89, 92, 100, 142n.13, 144n.31

Wolf, Immanuel, 83, 84

World History of the Jewish People, 95

Yabneh, 15, 16

Yemen, 32, 117

Yeven mezulah, 140n.41

Yom Kippur, 42

Yosippon, 34–35, 40, 61, 67

Za'ar bat rabbim, 140n.41

Zacuto, Abraham, 57, 58, 60, 63, 66

Zakhor ("remember"), 5

"Zarefat," 36

Zeitschrift für die Wissenschaft des Judenthums, 84

Zemaḥ David (David Gans), 58, 63

Zionism, 101

Zunz, Leopold, 83–84, 89

Zuq ha-'ittim, 140n.41